KT-430-265

How to Become a Police Officer

The ULTIMATE insider's guide to passing the

NEW Police Officer selection process

www.How2Become.com

Orders: Please contact How2Become Ltd, Suite 1, 60 Churchill Square Business Centre, Kings Hill, Kent ME19 4YU.

You can order through Amazon.co.uk under ISBN: 9781912370566, via the website www.How2Become.com or through Gardners.com.

ISBN: 9781912370566

First published 2018

Typeset for How2Become Ltd by Gemma Butler.

Disclaimer

Every effort has been made to ensure that the information contained within this guide is accurate at the time of publication. How2Become Ltd is not responsible for anyone failing any part of any selection process as a result of the information contained within this guide. How2Become Ltd and their authors cannot accept any responsibility for any errors or omissions within this guide, however caused. No responsibility for loss or damage occasioned by any person acting, or refraining from action, as a result of the material in this publication can be accepted by How2Become Ltd. The information within this guide does not represent the views of any third party service or organisation.

CONTENTS

The NEW Core Competencies 11

The Top 10 Insider Tips and Advice 27

Application Form...37

The New Police Assessment Centre 81

Assessment Centre Interview 165

Police Officer Assessment: Day Two............................193

Welcome to *How To Become A Police Officer.* This guide has been designed to help you prepare for, and pass, the tough police officer selection process.

As of 2018, the UK police have been piloting a new selection process, which has resulted in major transformation. From new competencies to entirely new selection tests and assessments, it's now harder than ever to join the UK police. Luckily, here at How2Become we are one step ahead of the game – and have produced this comprehensive guide. In this book we'll give you a FULL overview of the brand-new police officer selection process, and what it takes to pass.

> **IMPORTANT:** This guide is intended for the police forces that have opted for this new style selection process.
>
> It is also worth noting that this process is subject to slight changes as it is being piloted. However, the vast majority will likely remain the same and true to this book. Please be sure to check with your constabulary which process they are using before you apply!

The selection process to join the police is highly competitive. Approximately 65,000 people apply to join the police every year. But what is even more staggering is that only approximately 7,000 of those applicants will be successful.

You could view this as a worrying statistic, or alternatively you could view it that you are determined to be one of the 7,000 who are successful. Armed with this insider's guide, you have certainly taken the first step to passing the police officer selection process.

The guide itself has been split up into useful sections to make it easier for you to prepare for each stage. Read each section carefully and take notes as you progress. Don't ever give up on your dreams; if you really want to become a police officer then you can do it. The way to approach the police officer selection process is to embark on a programme of 'in-depth' preparation, and this guide will show you exactly how to do that.

The police officer selection process is not easy to pass, unless of course, you spend a decent amount of time preparing. Your preparation must be focused in the right areas, and also be comprehensive enough to give you every chance of success.

This guide will teach you how to be a successful candidate. The way to pass the police officer selection process is to develop your own skills and experiences around the **core competencies** that are required to become a police officer. However, now you also need to be aware of and understand the **values** and **clusters**, both of which will be important during the selection process. Many candidates who apply to join the police will be unaware that any of these three factors exist, and as a result they will have a huge disadvantage. As you progress through this guide, we'll show you how to focus your preparation around the values, clusters and core competencies, and how to use them during the assessment centre and interviews.

With the above in mind, the first step in your preparation is to start learning the core competencies, values and clusters. These will all form part of your application pack, but in the next chapter will give you a full break down of what these all are and how they should be used.

If you need any further help with any elements of the police officer selection process, aside from what is included within this guide, including role play, written tests and interview, then we offer a wide range of products to assist you. These are all available through our online shop www.How2Become.com. We also run a 1-day intensive police officer course. Details are available at the website www. PoliceCourse.co.uk.

Once again, thank you for your custom and we wish you every success in your pursuit of becoming a police officer.

Work hard, stay focused, and secure your dream job!

Best wishes,

The how2become team

The How2Become Team

PREFACE BY AUTHOR RICHARD MCMUNN

In 1993 I joined the Fire Service after serving four years in the Fleet Air Arm branch of the Royal Navy. After spending 16 successful years in the Fire Service, I decided to set up my own business and teach people like you how to prepare for a specific job. I have passed many different job applications and interviews during my life and I have also sat on the opposite side of the interview desk. Therefore, I have plenty of experience and knowledge that I will be sharing with you throughout this guide.

Throughout my career and working life I have always found that if I apply myself, and focus on the job in hand, then I will be successful. It is a formula that I have stuck with for many years, and it has always served me well. This kind of approach is one that I want to teach you over the forthcoming pages of this guide, and I hope that you will use my skills and knowledge to help you achieve the same levels of success that I have enjoyed.

Personally, I do not believe in luck when applying for jobs. I believe the candidates who successfully pass the police officer selection process do so because they thoroughly deserve it. They have prepared well and they have worked hard in order to improve their skills and knowledge.

I have always been a great believer in preparation. Preparation was my key to success, and it is also yours. Without the right level of preparation you will be setting out on the route to failure. The Police Service is very hard to join, but if you follow the steps that I have compiled within this guide then you will increase your chances of success dramatically. Remember, you are learning how to be a successful candidate, not a successful police officer!

The Police Service, like many other public services, has changed a great deal over the years and even more so in how it assesses potential candidates for police officer positions.

The men and women of the UK Police Service carry out an amazing job. They are there to protect the community in which they serve and they do that job with great pride, passion and very high levels of professionalism and commitment. They are to be congratulated for the service they provide.

Before you apply to join the Police Service you need to be fully confident that you too are capable of providing that same level of service. If you think you can do it, and you can rise to the challenge, then you just might be the type of person the police are looking for.

As you progress through this guide you will notice that the core competencies required to become a police officer are a common theme. You must learn these competencies, and also be able to demonstrate throughout the selection process, if you are to have any chance of successfully passing the selection process.

Finally, I have created a short video for you that provides details about a 1-day police officer training course I am running. You will find some useful tips and hints about passing the police selection process within the video too!

Here's a link to the video: www.PoliceCourse.co.uk

Best wishes

Richard McMunn

The NEW Core Competencies

As we mentioned in the first chapter, the UK police are now using a brand-new set of core competencies to evaluate candidates. Prior to 2018, you only needed to be aware of the core competencies, and how they link up with the role of a police officer. Now though, the game has changed quite dramatically. On top of brand new competencies, you'll also have to learn about two other behaviour groups – clusters and values.

In this chapter, we'll explain what all three of these elements mean, and how to use them.

Police Values

Similarly to the core competencies, the police values are a key part of the basic behavioural guidelines for any police employee. As one of the most esteemed and respected organisations in the world, the UK Police naturally have a number of values that they expect all candidates and employees to abide by, along with a strong code of ethics. In the past, the police have largely focused on the competencies of candidates rather than on their values as a person. While these values were still important, they played a secondary role. Now, the police are recognising that it's extremely important to hire candidates with strong values and ethics, and the new selection process is a reflection of this.

In accordance with the above, you can expect some of the interview questions to focus around your values, with questions such as:

'Can you tell me about a time when you've had to use good moral judgement, in a difficult scenario?'

'Can you tell me about a time when you've offered support to someone who needed it/someone who was vulnerable?'

The new police values are as follows:

Impartiality

Impartiality is all about staying true to the key principles of fairness and objectivity. It's absolutely vital that police officers can be impartial when dealing with members of the public, and with their colleagues. You must treat every single person that you meet with fairness and equal consideration, and be able to recognise and reprimand any and all forms of discrimination. Police officers must be able to put aside their personal feelings or beliefs, and make decisions with clear logic and rationale.

A police officer who can act with impartiality can:

- Understand the varying needs of individuals, and take these into account when making decisions.

- Treat every person in a fair and respectful manner.

- Ensure that they communicate effectively with everyone they meet, clearly relaying the message.

- Challenge prejudice and discrimination, whenever it arises.

- Make decisions using fair and objective reasoning.

- Value and appreciate the opinions of everyone whom they come into contact with, provided they are not in contradiction with the police code of ethics.

Integrity

Integrity is another extremely important part of the police code of ethics. Police officers must be able to act with integrity and decency at all times, and be capable of recognising both good and poor performance. As a police officer, your professionalism is absolutely integral. You are a representative of the police – a role model – and therefore it's fundamental that you can present an honest and trustworthy approach to the public. By doing this, you can build confidence from the public in the police force, and deliver a far more effective service.

A police officer with integrity can:

- Ensure that they behave in accordance with the police code of ethics, and make decisions that are focused on benefitting the public.

- Make decisions that will improve the reputation of the police, and understand their position as a role model within society.

- Welcome and take on board constructive criticism.

- Use their position of authority in society in a fair and professional manner, and as a force for positive change

Public Service

The third value on the list is public service. This value again links back to the police code of ethics, and is essentially about acting with the best interests of the public in mind. The police are there to protect the public, and safeguard them from harm. Therefore, it's important that your decisions are made with this aim in mind. You must be able to evaluate different strategies, how they will be of benefit to the wider public, and take responsibility to delivering upon these. Furthermore, public service is about facing up to challenges and adversity, and overcoming these obstacles, to provide a great level of service. You must be able to engage and communicate with the public, listening to their needs and making them feel valued and appreciated by the police.

A police officer with good public service can:

- Act with the bests interests of the public in mind.

- Put the needs of the public above your own interests.

- Adapt your communication to the appropriate audience.

- Make a conscious effort to understand the needs of different members of the public.

Transparency

Transparency is a really important quality for any police officer to have. This value is closely linked with honesty. It's essentially about being someone whom others can trust, and who others can have faith in. You must be able to explain, verbally and in writing, the rationale behind your decisions. You must be genuine with everyone you are communicating with, and make a concerted attempt to build trusting and strong relationships with your colleagues. Likewise, you must be someone who is capable of accepting criticism and improving your own working practice. It's very important that you can learn from and accept your own mistakes.

A police officer with transparency can:

- Be truthful, honest and tactful with others.

- Demonstrate an honest and critical approach to their own work, accepting that there are always areas for improvement.

- Take a clear and comprehensive approach to communicating with colleagues and members of the public.

- Behave in a way that invites members of the public, and your colleagues, to trust in you and your decision making.

- Understand and maintain confidentiality.

Looking at the values, you should be able to see that these are all basic behavioural qualities that you would expect from any police officer. During the selection process, it's likely that you'll be challenged on these values – through interview questions and various exercises, so make sure you study and learn them properly.

Next, we've got the clusters, which are closely linked with the core competencies.

Clusters

Clusters are essentially a group of core behaviours (hence cluster), which relate to the way in which a police officer should conduct themselves. There are three clusters in total, and under each cluster there are two competencies – so 6 competencies in total.

Below we've laid out the clusters and their related competencies. To make things easier, we've separated out the clusters and the competencies. Followed by each cluster, we've briefly mentioned which competencies it is linked with.

Resolute, Compassionate and Committed. This cluster relates to the way in which you conduct yourself as a police employee. Think about each of these terms, and what they mean, and how they relate to other vital personal qualities. For example, being compassionate means showing empathy for others, and demonstrating a high level of care and understanding for those around you. Once you learn to understand why people behave in the way that they do, you will be better equipped to understand the individual needs of different members of the public, and will be better placed to provide them with support. The better you can do this, the better it will reflect on the police as a whole.

This cluster links in with the core competencies of Emotional Awareness, and Taking Ownership.

Inclusive, Enabling And Visionary Leadership. Leadership is a very important quality for any police employee to have. All police employees must be able to motivate and encourage their colleagues, and members of the public, to speak out and help those around them. This is what 'inclusive' means, it's about helping everyone and getting everyone involved, not just particular people.

This cluster links in with the core competencies of Being Collaborative and Deliver, Support and Inspire.

Intelligent, Creative and Informed Policing. This cluster is all about being open to new ways of learning and development, to ensure that you are working to your maximum capacity. You must be able to think analytically, and form creative solutions to problems. Being informed means that you take every available factor into account before making a decision – you must take an evidence-based approach to problems, to ensure that every decision is made with sound logic and reasoning.

This cluster links in with the core competencies of Analysing Critically, and Being Innovative and Open Minded.

Core Competencies

Core competencies are a set of behavioural characteristics that all candidates to the police are expected to exhibit. These are behavioural qualities that you will 16

need to demonstrate on a constant basis while working as a police officer, and therefore it's vital for the police to establish that you understand them, and have previously demonstrated them in the past.

There are three levels to each core competency, with the third level being the most advanced.

Emotionally Aware

It's very important for police officers to be emotionally aware. Not only do you need to be emotionally aware towards the needs and feelings of others, but you also need to be emotionally aware of yourself. You must be able to control your emotions when under high amounts of pressure, and exhibit strong levels of decision making. Police work is highly stressful, and will push you to your limits. Therefore, it's vital that police employees can stay calm and collected, and manage their emotions.

Level 1: Emotional Awareness

Level 1 is the most basic level of the competency. At Level 1, candidates must exhibit qualities such as:

- Treating others with respect and compassion.

- Acknowledging other people's opinions, values and beliefs – provided they fall within lawful boundaries.

- Asking for help when necessary.

- Recognising your own limitations, and seeking assistance in accordance with this.

Level 2: Emotional Awareness

Level 2 is a slightly more advanced level of the competency. At Level 2, candidates must exhibit qualities such as:

- Adapting their approach to the needs of specific/different individuals.

- Promoting diversity and valuing the different qualities of individual colleagues.

- Encouraging others to reflect on their own work, and supporting them to improve.

- Taking responsibility for the emotional welfare of other members of your team.

Level 3: Emotional Awareness

Level 3 is the most advanced level of the competency. At Level 3, candidates must exhibit qualities such as:

- Understanding the reasons behind certain organisational behaviour requirements, and playing a key role in adapting and improving these expectations when necessary.

- Using their influence in an effective and professional manner, to help resolve internal issues within the police force.

- Viewing police work through a variety of spectrums, and being able to challenge your own views and assumptions.

Taking Ownership

In order to work as a police officer, it's vital that you can take ownership and responsibility, and hold yourself accountable for your own actions. Part of this means accepting that sometimes minor mistakes will happen, but the way you deal with these is what is important. You must learn from your mistakes, and seek improvement-based feedback. Furthermore, it's critical that you can take pride in your work, and recognise your own limitations.

Level 1: Taking Ownership

Level 1 is the most basic level of the competency. At Level 1, candidates must exhibit qualities such as:

- Accurately identifying and then responding to problems/issues.

- Completing tasks with enthusiasm and positivity.

- Taking responsibility for their own decisions.

- Providing others with helpful and constructive feedback on their working practice.

Level 2: Taking Ownership

Level 2 is a slightly more advanced level of the competency. At Level 2, candidates must exhibit qualities such as:

- Promoting an internal and external culture of ownership and responsibility, so that your colleagues can take responsibility for their own decisions.

- Play an active role in making improvements to the police force, through regular examination of police policies and procedures, to ensure that the service is operating to its maximum potential.

- Taking accountability for the decisions that other members of your team make.

- Taking personal responsibility for correcting problems that you notice within the force.

Level 3: Taking Ownership

Level 3 is the most advanced level of the competency. At Level 3, candidates must exhibit qualities such as:

- Embracing the idea of being a role model, and using mistakes and errors as a learning process and a chance for improvement.

- Helping to instigate measures that will allow others to take responsibility in a more effective and smooth fashion.

- Looking at issues from a wider police perspective, and how they will impact the reputation of the service as a whole.

- Being someone whom others can look up to, in order to see the excellent and all-encompassing standards and values of the UK police.

Working Collaboratively

Teamwork is a fundamental part of working as a police officer, and the better you can work as part of a collaborative unit, the better level of service you can provide to the public. Good police work is about building partnerships, not just with your colleagues, but with members of the public too. You must be polite and respectful with every person that you meet, and show that the police value the ideals of teamwork, collaboration and social unity.

Level 1: Working Collaboratively

Level 1 is the most basic level of the competency. At Level 1, candidates must exhibit qualities such as:

- Working cooperatively and in harmony with colleagues and professionals from other organisations.

- Exhibiting an approachable and friendly exterior, so that others feel comfortable asking you for help or guidance.

- Showing a genuine interest and appreciation in other people, their views and opinions, in order to build comradery and rapport.

- Treating every person that you meet as an individual.

Level 2: Working Collaboratively

Level 2 is a slightly more advanced level of the competency. At Level 2, candidates must exhibit qualities such as:

- Managing the relationship between the police service and partnership organisations, with the aim of producing long-term benefits for the general public.

- Working with partnership organisations, to create public welfare initiatives.

- Communicate effectively with everyone whom they come into contact with.

- Work amicably and professionally with members of the public, to build trust in the police service.

Level 3: Working Collaboratively

Level 3 is the most advanced level of the competency. At Level 3, candidates must exhibit qualities such as:

- Demonstrating political awareness, and an understanding of how politics can impact on the relationship between the police and their partnership agencies.

- Helping others to build relationships with external potential partnership organisations, which could be of benefit to the police and the general public.

- Setting the standard for the way in which partnership organisations interact with and work with the police service.

- Helping to create an environment that is conducive to partnership work.

Deliver, Support and Inspire

It's imperative that police officers understand the wider vision of the police service. You must use the police's values in your day-to-day work, and show a dedication to working in the best interests of the public. Your positive contribution to the police is extremely important. Police officers must show an understanding of how their behaviour impacts on the reputation of the service, and strive to make a positive contribution to this at all times. You must be focused on helping your teammates to achieve high standards, whilst maintaining your own.

Level 1: Deliver, Support and Inspire

Level 1 is the most basic level of the competency. At Level 1, candidates must exhibit qualities such as:

- Being willing and ready to tackle challenging tasks, with the aim of improving the output of the police service.

- Demonstrating an understanding of how their work contributes to the police as a whole.

- Taking a conscientious and resilient approach to police work, always endeavouring to provide the best possible service.

- Using resources efficiently, to make a significant impact.

Level 2: Deliver, Support and Inspire

Level 2 is a slightly more advanced level of the competency. At Level 2, candidates must exhibit qualities such as:

-   Giving clear instructions to others, and helping colleagues to understand how their work impacts the wider police service.

-   Breaking down potential barriers to optimal performance.

-   Providing advice and support to the public and to your colleagues.

-   Using resources in the most appropriate and efficient manner, to deliver a significant impact.

-   Motivating others, and inspiring them to achieve success and maintain high standards.

Level 3: Deliver, Support and Inspire

Level 3 is the most advanced level of the competency. At Level 3, candidates must exhibit qualities such as:

-   Constantly challenging others to maintain the vision of the police service, to the highest possible standards.

-   Making conscious efforts to demonstrate to your colleagues about how specific tasks and ideas link in with the wider vision of the police.

-   Helping others to understand their individual goals, comprehensibly, and how these goals fit in with the wider vision of the police.

-   Monitoring changes, both internally and externally, and take steps to guarantee positive outcomes.

-   Thinking in a strategic and detailed fashion, demonstrating long-term planning and knowledge.

Analyse Critically

Working as a police officer involves large amount of critical analysis. You'll be presented with a wide variety of data, and will need to use all of this data to come to informed decisions. This is essentially what 'taking an evidence-based approach' means. It's about using the evidence available to you effectively and efficiently, to gather as many facts and hard info as possible, before using this data in the most logical way.

Level 1: Analyse Critically

Level 1 is the most basic level of the competency. At Level 1, candidates must exhibit qualities such as:

- Understanding the importance of critical thinking, analysis and careful consideration before making decisions.

- Assessing and analysing information in an efficient and accurate manner.

- Solving problems by using logic and sound reasoning.

- Balancing out the advantages and disadvantages of actions, before taking them.

- Recognising and pointing out flaws in data or information.

Level 2: Analyse Critically

Level 2 is a slightly more advanced level of the competency. At Level 2, candidates must exhibit qualities such as:

- Taking information from a wide range of sources into consideration, before making decisions.

- Understanding the long-term consequences of potential actions.

- Recognising when the right time to take action is, and understanding how to limit the risks involved in said action.

- Encouraging others to make decisions in line with the police code of ethics.

Level 3: Analyse Critically

Level 3 is the most advanced level of the competency. At Level 3, candidates must exhibit qualities such as:

-   Balancing out the risks and benefits of all decisions, with consideration on the wider impact of said decisions.

-   Understanding it's appropriate to raise concerns or challenge decisions made by those in a senior position to you.

-   Using your knowledge of the wider policing to inform your decisions.

-   Being willing to make difficult decisions, even if these decisions could result in significant change.

Innovative and Open Minded

The final competency challenges the mindset of the candidate. It's extremely important that you can take an open-minded approach to police work. Not everything is straightforward and 'by the book'. There will always be problems which require an innovative and creative solution, and it's your job to come up with this! Furthermore, it's essential that you can take an open mind to new ways of working, and understand that continuous development is a necessity for any police officer.

Level 1: Innovative and Open Minded

Level 1 is the most basic level of the competency. At Level 1, candidates must exhibit qualities such as:

-   Being openness to new perspectives, ideas and perceptions.

-   Sharing ideas and suggestions with colleagues, with the aim of improving current police practice.

-   Reflecting on their own working practice and how it can be improved.

-   Adapting to changing circumstances and needs.

Level 2: Innovative and Open Minded

Level 2 is a slightly more advanced level of the competency. At Level 2, candidates must exhibit qualities such as:

- Using a number of different sources to gain information, using common sense, and not 'just' police criteria.

- Identifying potential barriers or problems which could present an obstacle to the way in which you and your colleagues work in the future.

- Taking a flexible approach to problems, being willing to adapt and change when necessary.

- Encouraging others to think creatively and take risks where it is right.

Level 3: Innovative and Open Minded

Level 3 is the most advanced level of the competency. At Level 3, candidates must exhibit qualities such as:

- Implementing new ways of working, which can have a significant positive change on future working practice.

- Encouraging others to review their own performance through the lens of long-term policing.

- Playing a central role in developing a positive learning culture, taking steps to promote innovation and creativity.

- Taking part in creating new initiatives, with police partnership agencies.

- Taking accountability for improvement and change within the police force.

Why have these been implemented?

So, why all the new changes? Well, fundamentally, the police wanted to design a set of competencies that are a more accurate reflection on actual police work. The new competencies/clusters/

values not only provide all police employees with a clearer set of ethics and information on exactly how they should behave, but they also provide clearer information on how frontline and non-frontline police employees should behave. Instead of having 'all-encompassing' competencies, now every single person in the police can see exactly what is expected of them, and in what way.

How will they be used?

The selection process to join the police involves a large number of different tests and assessments. The majority of these assessments will directly challenge your skills in dealing with people. You'll face role-play assessments, tests where you need to respond verbally or in writing to another member of the colleague, and tests where you need to work closely with colleagues. Throughout all of these exercises, you will be required to demonstrate your understanding and knowledge of the above behavioural traits and qualities. You will be scored based on how well you can exhibit and demonstrate these, so make sure you learn them thoroughly and well in advance of the selection process.

Before we move onto the application form, please allow us to give you some top insider tips, which will prove extremely useful on your police recruitment journey.

The Top 10 Insider Tips and Advice

The following 10 insider tips have been carefully put together to increase your chances of success during the police officer selection process. Therefore, it is important that you follow them carefully. Whilst some of them will appear obvious, they are still important tips which you need to follow.

INSIDER TIP 1 – BE FULLY PREPARED AND FOCUSED

When you are applying for any career it is of vital importance that you prepare yourself fully for every stage of the selection process. Do everything you can to find out what is required of you. For example, most people do not read the guidance notes that accompany the application form, and then they wonder why they fail that particular section.

Make sure you read every all of the information you receive at least twice and understand what is required in order to pass. Much in life does not come easy and you must be prepared to work hard. Go out of your way to prepare – for example, get a friend or relative to act out a role play scenario and see how you deal with it. When completing the application form allocate plenty of time to do it neatly, concisely and correctly. Don't leave it until the night before the closing date to fill out the form, as you will be setting yourself out to fail.

We will talk about 'preparation' on many occasions throughout this guide and you should make sure you take on board our advice.

Break down your preparation into the following 4 key areas:

Area 1 – Learn about the role of a police officer.

Area 2 – Learn and understand the core competencies.

Area 3 – Prepare to apply the core competencies to every stage of the selection process.

Area 4 – Improve your physical fitness.

In addition to your preparation strategy, it is also very important to believe in your own abilities and take advantage of the potential that's within you. If you work hard then you will be rewarded!

Whenever you come up against hurdles or difficult situations and experiences, always try to look for the opportunity to improve yourself. For example, if you have applied for the police previously and failed, what have you done to improve your chances of success the second time around? Did you find out what areas you failed on and have you done anything to improve?

INSIDER TIP 2 – UNDERSTAND AND BELIEVE IN EQUALITY AND FAIRNESS, AND BE ABLE TO DEMONSTRATE IT DURING THE SELECTION PROCESS

Equality and fairness are crucial in today's society. We must treat each other with respect and dignity, and understand that people come from different backgrounds and cultures to our own.

Treat people how you expect to be treated – with dignity and respect. If you do not believe in equality, fairness and dignity, then you are applying for the wrong job. Police officers are role models within society and people will look to you to set an example. For example, you wouldn't expect to see a police officer bullying or shouting at a member of the public in an aggressive manner, would you? As a police officer you will only use force in exceptional circumstances. You will be required to use your interpersonal skills to diffuse situations and you will need to treat people fairly and equally at all times.

INSIDER TIP 3 – BE PHYSICALLY AND MENTALLY FIT

Being prepared, both physically and mentally, is important if you are to succeed in your application to become a police officer. Even if you only have a few weeks to prepare, there are lots of ways in which you can improve your chances of success.

Many people who successfully pass the selection process are physically fit. Being physically fit has plenty of advantages in addition to simply improving your health. For example, raised self-esteem and confidence in your appearance are also benefits to keeping fit. A person with good health and fitness generally shines when it comes to how they look, how they treat others, and how they go about their day-to-day activities.

In addition to the above, the benefits of 'fitness of mind' are equally as important when tackling the selection process.

When applying to join the police you will be learning new skills and developing old ones. The fitter your mind, the easier this will be. If you are fit, both physically and mentally, then you will be able to prepare for longer. You will find that your stamina levels will increase and therefore your ability to practise and prepare will increase too.

If you prepare yourself fully for the selection process then you will feel more confident on the day, when you are under pressure. Make sure you also get plenty of sleep in the build up to selection and ensure you eat a healthy balanced diet. Many of us underestimate the importance of a healthy diet.

The saying 'we are what we eat' makes a lot of sense and you will find that if you just spend a week or two eating and drinking the right things you will begin to look and feel healthier. Avoid junk food, alcohol and cigarettes during your preparation and your concentration levels will increase greatly, helping you to get the most out of the work you put in. Give yourself every opportunity to succeed!

INSIDER TIP 4 – LEARN ABOUT THE POLICE SERVICE YOU ARE APPLYING TO JOIN

This is important for a number of reasons. To begin with, you may be asked a question on the application form that relates to your knowledge of the role of a police officer and also why you want to join that particular constabulary. As you can appreciate, many candidates will apply for a number of different constabularies all at once in an attempt to secure a job as a police officer. The Police Service you are applying to join wants to know what exactly attracts you to them. In order to be able to provide a good response to this type of question, you will need to carry out some research.

The second reason is that some Police Services are now holding 'final interviews', which are in addition to the standard competency based assessment centre interview. During this interview it is guaranteed that you will be asked questions relating to your knowledge of the service.

Most Police Services have a website. Visit their website and find out what they are doing in terms of community policing. Remember that the job of a police officer is not just about catching criminals. It is about delivering the best possible service to the public and responding to their needs. Understanding what the police in your area are trying to achieve will demonstrate enthusiasm, commitment and an understanding of what your job will involve if you are successful.

If you can tell the interview panel about the policing area, current crime trends and statistics, community policing issues and even diversity recruitment, then you will be displaying a far greater knowledge of their constabulary and also showing them that you have made the effort!

If you were interviewing a candidate for employment in your Police Service, what would you expect them to know about your organisation? You would probably expect them to know a great deal of information. Learn as much information as possible about the service you are applying to join and be extremely thorough in your preparation.

INSIDER TIP 5 – LEARN AND UNDERSTAND THE CORE COMPETENCIES

VERY IMPORTANT – DO NOT IGNORE

The police officer core competencies form the fundamental requirements of the role. They identify how you should perform and they are key to the role of a police officer. Read them carefully and make sure you understand them, they are crucial to your success!

Throughout the selection process you should concentrate on the core competencies, constantly trying to demonstrate them at every stage.

When completing the application form your answers should be based around the core competencies. The same rule applies to the written tests, the interview and also the role play exercises. The most effective way to achieve this is to use 'keywords and phrases' in your responses to the application form and interview questions.

You can also adopt this method when tackling the role plays and the written tests. Using keywords and phrases that correspond to the core competencies will gain you higher scores. Within this guide we will show you how to achieve this, but the first step is for you to learn the core competencies.

Make sure you have a copy of the competencies next to you when completing the application form and whilst preparing for the assessment centre.

This is the most important tip we can provide you with – Do not ignore it!

INSIDER TIP 6 – BE PATIENT AND LEARN FROM YOUR MISTAKES

We can all become impatient when we really want something in life but sometimes it may take us a little longer than expected to reach our goals.

Try to understand that the Police Service receives many thousands of applications each year and it takes time for them to process each one. Don't contact the Police Service with a view to chasing up your application but rather wait for them to get in touch with you. Use the time in between your results wisely, concentrating on the next stage of the selection process. For example, as soon as you submit your application form, start working on your preparation for the assessment centre. 99% of candidates will not start their preparation for the assessment centre until they receive their results. They can't be bothered to prepare for the next stage until they receive confirmation that they've been successful, and as a result, they are missing out on a few extra weeks of practise time.

Remember that you are applying to join a job that will pay you a salary of approximately £30,000 a year! That is worth studying hard for. So, use every bit of spare time you get wisely by not sitting around in between results but rather using that time to prepare for the next stage.

If you have previously been through selection then it is crucial that you find out why you failed. This will allow you to improve for next time. You should receive a feedback form from the Police Service informing you of which areas you need to improve on. It is pointless going through selection again unless you improve on your weak areas, as you will simply make the same mistakes again.

INSIDER TIP 7 – UNDERSTAND DIVERSITY AND THE BENEFITS IT BRINGS TO A WORKFORCE AND SOCIETY

A diverse community has great benefits and the same can be said for a diverse workforce.

The Police Service is no exception and it needs to represent the community in which it serves. If society itself is multicultural, then the Police Service needs to be too.

Ask yourself the question "What is diversity?" If you cannot answer this then you need to find out. You will almost certainly be asked a question about it during the application form stage and the final interview, if applicable.

The Police Service must uphold the law fairly and appropriately to protect, respect, help and reassure everyone in all communities. The Police Service must also meet all of the current legislative requirements concerning human rights, race, disability and all employment law that relates to equality.

The focus of the Police Service is to provide a service that responds to the needs of all communities, ensuring the promotion of fair working practices at all times. The concept of diversity encompasses acceptance and respect. It means understanding that each individual is unique, and recognising our individual differences. These can be along the dimensions of race, ethnicity, gender, sexual orientation, socio-economic status, age, physical abilities, religious beliefs, political beliefs, or other ideologies. It is about understanding each other and moving beyond simple tolerance to embracing and celebrating the rich dimensions of diversity contained within each individual.

Learn, understand and believe in diversity. It is important during the selection process and even more important in relation to your role as a police officer.

INSIDER TIP 8 – DO NOT GIVE UP UNTIL YOU HAVE REACHED YOUR GOAL

If you don't reach the required standard at the first or subsequent attempts, don't give up. So long as you always try to better yourself, there is always the chance that you will succeed. If you do fail any of the stages, look at the area(s) you need to improve on.

Did you fail the fitness test? If so then there are ways of improving. Don't just sit back and wait for the next opportunity to come along, prepare for it straight away and you'll increase your chances for next time.

Many people give up on their goals far too easily. Learning to find the positive aspects in negative situations is a difficult thing to do, but is a skill that anyone can acquire through practice and determination.

If you really want to achieve your goals then anything is possible. During your preparation set yourself small targets each week. For example, your first week may be used to concentrate on learning the core competencies. Your second week can be used to prepare for your written responses on the application form and so on.

If you get tired or feel de-motivated at any time during your preparation, walk away from it and give yourself a break. You may find that you come back to it re-energised, more focused and determined to succeed!

INSIDER TIP 9 – PRACTICE THE ROLE PLAY EXERCISES WITH A FRIEND OR RELATIVE

The role play scenarios can be a daunting experience, especially if you've never done anything like this before. Whilst the Police Service will advise you to be yourself, there are ways in which you can prepare and subsequently increase your chances of success.

The way to prepare for the role plays is to act them out in a room with a friend or relative. Within this guide you have been provided with a number of example role play scenarios. Use these to practise with, and hone your skills in each area of the core competencies that are being assessed.

The only way that you will be able to understand what is required during the role play exercises is to learn the assessable core competencies. For example, if you are being assessed against the core competency of service delivery, then you will need to demonstrate the following during each role play scenario:

- Be professional and present an appropriate image in line with your brief and job description.

- Focus on the needs of the customer in every scenario.

- Sort out any problems as soon as possible and apologise for any errors or mistakes that have been made.

- Ask the customer whether they are satisfied with your actions or not. If they are not, then take alternative steps to make them satisfied if possible.

- Keep the customer updated on progress.

Doing all of the above, in addition to covering the other assessable areas, can be quite a difficult task. However, if you practise these skills regularly in the build-up to your assessment then you will find it becomes easier and easier the more that you do.

INSIDER TIP 10 – PRACTISE A MOCK INTERVIEW

Mock interviews are a fantastic way to prepare for both the assessment centre interview, and also the final interview, if applicable.

During the build-up to interviews, write down a number of predicted interview questions that you have created during your research. Then ask a friend or relative to ask you these questions under formal interview conditions. This is excellent preparation, and will serve you well during all of your career interviews.

We also strongly recommend that you sit down in front of a long mirror and respond to the same set of interview questions. Watch your interview technique. Do you slouch? Do you fidget and do you overuse your hands? It is important that you work on your interview technique during the build-up to the assessment centre and the final interview.

Do not make the mistake of carrying out little or no preparation, because you can be guaranteed that some of the other candidates will have prepared fully. Make sure you put in the time and effort and practise a number of mock interviews. You will be amazed at how confident you will feel during the real interview.

BONUS TIP – CONSIDER CARRYING OUT SOME COMMUNITY WORK

Demonstrating that you are capable of working effectively in the community before you join the police will give you a positive edge over other candidates. Being able to add this information to your application and also at the interview stage will make you stand out from the rest of the competition.

Why not organise a small charity event in your local area? Maybe a sponsored swim, cycle ride or car wash? The reason why we advise undertaking this type of project is that it gives you more relevant experiences to draw on during the selection process.

If you organise such an event on your own or as a team then it demonstrates your ability to organise and solve problems, which are key police officer core competencies. It also demonstrates that you are a caring person and that you are prepared to go out of your way to help others. You may also get fit in the process!

Other effective ways of working in the community are either through neighbourhood watch schemes, becoming a special constable, part-time firefighter or carrying out any form of voluntary work. Make the effort and go out on a limb to stand out from the rest of the applicants.

Now that we have taken a look at the top insider tips and advice, let us now put all that we have learnt so far into practice. The first step is the successful completion of the application form.

Application Form

The application form is the first stage of the selection process for becoming a police officer. During this section we will provide you with a step by step approach to completing a successful application. It is important to point out that we have used a number of the more common types of application form questions within this section and it is your responsibility to confirm that they relate to your particular form. We have deliberately not made reference to any sections of the form that relate to personal details, simply because what you write here is based on you and you alone.

We recommend you allow at least five evenings to complete the form, breaking it up into manageable sections. Many candidates will try and complete the form in one sitting and as a result their concentration will wane and so will the quality of their submission.

You will be asked a number of questions on the application form and on the following pages we have provided you with some tips and advice on how to approach these questions. Please remember that these are provided as a guide only and you should base your answers around your own experiences in both work life and personal life. Questions that are based around 'knowledge, skills and experience' are looking for you to demonstrate that you can meet the requirements of the 'person specification' for the job you are applying for. Therefore, your answer should match these as closely as possible. Your first step is to find out what the 'person specification' is for the particular constabulary you are applying to join.

As we have explained, the role of a police officer is made up of a number of core competencies. You may receive these in your application pack or alternatively they can usually be found on the website of the service you are applying to join. Whatever you do, make sure you get a copy of them, and have them by your side when completing the application form. Basically you are looking to match your responses with the police officer core competencies.

Once you have found the 'core competencies', now is the time to structure your answers around these, ensuring that you briefly cover each area based upon your own experiences in both your work life and personal life.

Before we get started with the questions, take a read of the following important tips, which will help you to submit a first-class application.

*   Make sure you read the whole of the application form at least twice before preparing your responses, including the guidance notes.

*   Read and understand the person specification and the police officer core competencies.

*   Try to tailor your answers around the 'core competencies' and include any keywords or phrases you think are relevant.

*   Make sure you base your answers on actual events that you have experienced either in your work life or personal life.

*   Fill the form out in the correct ink colour. If you fail to follow this simple instruction then your form may end up in the bin!

*   If there is a specific word count for each question, make sure you stick to it.

*   Do not lie.

*   Get someone to read your practice/completed application form to check for spelling/grammar mistakes. You lose marks for poor grammar/spelling.

*   Answer all of the questions to the best of your ability. If you leave a question blank, it is highly unlikely you will move on to the next stage.

*   Follow the prompts given in each question. They will help to give your answers a clearer structure.

*   Use examples from your work, social, domestic or educational life to answer the questions. In these examples, they are looking for evidence of specific behaviours which research has shown to be essential to police work.

*   Be specific: they want to know what YOU said or did on a given occasion to deal with the situation. It's therefore important that

the examples you provide are your own experiences and as detailed as possible.

- Try to use examples that you found difficult or challenging to deal with. These answers tend to achieve better marks.

- Write clearly and concisely. They expect your answers to be focused, succinct and fluently written, as any police report or statement would need to be. This means writing in complete sentences rather than notes or bullet points.

- Pay attention to your handwriting, spelling, punctuation and grammar. Remember this is a formal application so the use of jargon and slang is unacceptable.

- Do not add extra sheets, write outside the space provided or write between the lines. No marks will be given for evidence outside the space provided.

- Most constabularies will give you the option to submit the form digitally. However, if you are intending to send it via post, then make sure you use recorded delivery. This will prevent your form going missing, which happens more often than you would think.

SAMPLE APPLICATION FORM QUESTIONS AND RESPONSES

The following sample application form questions may not be applicable to your specific form. However, they will provide you with some excellent tips and advice on how to approach the questions.

SAMPLE QUESTION NUMBER 1

Q. What knowledge, skills and experiences do you have that will enable you to meet the requirements of a police officer?

ANSWER (EXAMPLE ONLY)

"In my previous employment as a customer services assistant I was required to work closely with the general public on many occasions. Often I would be required to provide varied solutions to customers' problems or complaints after listening to their concerns. It was always important for me to listen carefully to what they had to say and respond in a manner that was both respectful and understanding.

On some occasions I would have to communicate with members of the public from a different race or background and I made sure I paid particular attention to making sure they understood how I was going to resolve their problems.

I would always be sensitive to how they may have been feeling on the other end of the telephone. Every Monday morning the team that I was a part of would hold a meeting to discuss ways in which we could improve our service to the customer. During these meetings I would always ensure that I contributed and shared any relevant experiences I had during the previous week. Sometimes during the group discussions I would find that some members of the group were shy and not very confident at coming forward, so I always sensitively tried to involve them wherever possible.

I remember on one occasion during a meeting I provided a solution to a problem that had been on-going for some time. I had noticed that customers would often call back to see if their complaint had been resolved, which was often time-consuming for the company to deal with. So I suggested that we should have a system where customers were called back after 48 hours with an update of progress in relation to their complaint. My suggestion was taken forward and is now an integral part of the company's procedures. I found it quite hard at first to persuade managers to take on my idea but I was confident that the change would provide a better service to the public we were serving."

Although the question here has not directly referenced a competency, the police will expect you to identify which competency is most relevant here, and then apply it to your answer. So, in this case, the question is asking you to demonstrate the core competency of **deliver, support and inspire.**

Hopefully you are now beginning to understand what is required and how important it is to 'match' your response with the core competencies that are being assessed. Remember to make sure you read fully the guidance notes that are contained within your application pack. You will also hopefully start to realise why we recommend you set aside five evenings to complete the form!

It is also possible to use examples from your personal life, so don't just think about work experiences but look at other aspects of your life too. Try also to think of any community work that you have been involved in. Have you been a special constable or do you work for a charity or other similar organisation? Maybe you are a member of neighbourhood watch and if so you should find it quite a simple process to match the core competencies.

We have now provided a number of sample keywords and phrases that are relevant to each core competency. These will help you to understand exactly what we mean when we say 'match' the core competencies in each of your responses.

Emotionally Aware

✓   I treated the customer with respect and compassion.

✓   I addressed the needs of the person I was dealing with.

✓   I realised that I needed to control my own emotions.

✓   By speaking with them on a personal level, I was able to build their confidence in my abilities.

✓ I took the time to identify the best way to meet their needs.

✓ I understood how they might have been feeling about this situation.

Taking Ownership

✓ I am happy to make big decisions and take responsibility when required.

✓ I take responsibility for the actions of my colleagues and teammates.

✓ I complete tasks with enthusiasm and positivity.

✓ I embrace the idea of being a role model.

✓ I understand when it is the right time to take advice from others.

Working Collaboratively

✓ I worked with the other members of the team to get the task completed.

✓ At all times I considered the other members of the team and offered my support whenever possible.

✓ I took steps to develop a positive working relationship with the other members of the team.

✓ I fully briefed the other members of the team on what we need to achieve.

✓ I adapted my style of communication to fit the audience.

✓ I listened to the other person's views and took them into consideration.

✓ I took positive steps to persuade the team to follow my course of action.

✓ I kept the others updated of my progress at all times.

Deliver, Support and Inspire

✓ I acted at all times in a professional and ethical manner.

✓ I took responsibility for solving the problem.

✓ I stood by my decision despite the objections from others.

✓ I remained calm at all times and in control of the situation.

✓ I immediately challenged the inappropriate behaviour.

✓ In order to improve my performance I sought feedback from my manager.

✓ I took steps to defuse the conflict.

✓ I took control of the situation in order to achieve a positive outcome.

Analyse Critically

✓ I gathered all of the information available before making my decision.

✓ I verified that the information was accurate before using it to make a decision.

✓ I considered all possible options first.

✓ I reviewed my decision once the new information had become available.

✓ I considered the wider implications before making my decision.

✓ I remained impartial at all times.

✓ I considered the confidentiality of the information I was receiving.

Innovative and Open Minded

✓ I was positive about the pending change.

✓ I took steps to adapt to the new working-practices.

✓ I put in extra effort to make the changes work.

✓ I was flexible in my approach to work.

✓ I searched for alternative ways to deal with the situation.

✓ I took an innovative approach to working with the new guidelines and procedures.

You will notice that we have used the word 'I' many times during the above sample keywords and phrases. This is deliberate. Remember, it is important that you explain what YOU did during your responses.

Now let's move on to some more sample application form interview questions and responses.

SAMPLE QUESTION NUMBER 2

Q. Why have you applied for this post and what do you have to offer?

Some Police Service application forms may ask you questions based around the question above. If so, then you need to answer again in conjunction with the 'person spec' relevant to that particular constabulary.

An example answer for the above question could be based around the following:

"I believe my personal qualities and attributes would be suited to that of a police officer within this Constabulary. I enjoy working in a diverse organisation that offers many and varied challenges. I would enjoy the challenge of working in a public service environment that requires a high level of personal responsibility, openness to change and working with others. I have a high level of commitment, motivation and integrity, which I believe would help the Police Service respond to the needs of their community."

Top tips

- The length of response that you provide should be dictated by the amount of space available to you on the application form or the specified number of maximum words.

- The form itself may provide you with the facility to attach a separate sheet if necessary. If it doesn't then make sure you keep to the space provided.

- The best tip we can give you is to write down your answer first in rough before committing your answer to paper on the actual application form. This will allow you to correct any errors.

SAMPLE QUESTION NUMBER 3

Q. It is essential that police officers are capable of showing respect for other people regardless of their background.

Please describe a situation when you have challenged someone's behaviour that was bullying, discriminatory or insensitive. You will be assessed on how positively you acted during the situation, and also on how well you understood what had occurred.

PART 1 – Describe the situation and also tell us about the other person or people who were involved.

"Whilst working as a sales person for my previous employer, I was serving a lady who was from an ethnic background. I was helping her to choose a gift for her son's 7th birthday when a group of four youths entered the shop and began looking around at the goods we had for sale.

For some strange reason they began to make racist jokes and comments to the lady. I was naturally offended by the comments and was concerned for the lady to whom these comments were directed.

Any form of bullying and harassment is not welcome in any situation and I was determined to stop it immediately and protect the lady from any more harm."

Top tips

- Try to answer this type of question focusing on the positive action that you took, identifying that you understood the situation. Don't forget to include keywords and phrases in your response that are relevant to the competencies that are being assessed.

- Make sure you are honest in your responses. The situations you provide MUST be real and ones that you took part in.

PART 2 – What did you say and what did you do?

"The lady was clearly upset by their actions and I too found them both offensive and insensitive. I decided to take immediate action and stood between the lady and the youths to try to protect her from any more verbal abuse or comments. I told them in a calm manner that their comments were not welcome and would not be tolerated. I then called over my manager for assistance and asked him to call the police before asking the four youths to leave the shop.

I wanted to diffuse the situation as soon as possible, being constantly aware of the lady's feelings. I was confident that the shop's CCTV cameras would have picked up the four offending youths and that the police would be able to deal with the situation.

After the youths had left the shop I sat the lady down and made her a cup of tea whilst we waited for the police to arrive. I did everything that I could to support and comfort the lady and told her that I would be prepared to act as a witness to the bullying and harassment that I had just witnessed."

Top tip

- Remember to read the core competencies before constructing your response. What are the police looking for in relation to what YOU say to others and how you act?

PART 3 – Why do you think the other people behaved as they did?

"I believe it is predominantly down to a lack of understanding, education and awareness. Unless people are educated and understand why these comments are not acceptable then they are not open to change.

They behave in this manner because they are unaware of how dangerous their comments and actions are. They believe it is socially acceptable to act this way when it certainly isn't."

Top tip

- When describing your thoughts or opinions on how others acted in a given situation, keep your personal views separate. Try to provide a response that shows a mature understanding of the situation.

PART 4 – What would have been the consequences if you had not acted as you did?

"The consequences are numerous. To begin with I would have been condoning this type of behaviour and missing an opportunity to let the offenders know that their actions are wrong (educating them). I would have also been letting the lady down, which would have in turn made her feel frightened, hurt and not supported.

We all have the opportunity to help stop discriminatory behaviour and providing we ourselves are not in any physical danger then we should take positive action to stop it."

Top tip

- Try to demonstrate an understanding of what would have possibly happened if you had failed to take action.

SAMPLE QUESTION NUMBER 4

Q. Police officers are required to work in teams and therefore they must be able to work well with others. Please describe a situation when it was necessary to work with other people in order to get something done and achieve a positive result. During this question you will be assessed on how you cooperated with the other members of the team in completing the task in hand.

PART 1 – Tell us what had to be done.

"Whilst driving along the motorway I noticed that an accident had just occurred in front of me. Two cars were involved in the accident and some people in the car appeared to be injured. There were a number of people stood around looking at the crash and I was concerned that help had not been called.

We needed to work as a team to call the emergency services, look after the injured people in the cars and try to stay as safe as possible."

Top tip

- Make sure you provide a response to the questions that is specific in nature. Do not fall into the trap of telling them what you 'would do' if the situation was to occur. Tell them what you DID do.

PART 2 – How was it that you became involved?

"I became involved through pure instinct. I'm not the type of person to sit in the background and let others resolve situations. I prefer to try to help out where I can and I believed that, in this situation, something needed to be done. It was apparent that people were hurt and the emergency services had not been called yet. There were plenty of people around but they weren't working as a team to get the essentials done."

Top tip

- It is better to say that you volunteered to get involved rather than that you were asked.

PART 3 – What did you do and what did others do?

"I immediately shouted out loud and asked if anybody was a trained first aid person, nurse or doctor. A man came running over and told me that he worked for the British Red Cross and that he had a first aid kit in his car. He told me that he would look after the injured people but that he would need an assistant. I asked a lady if she would help him and she said that she would. I then decided that I needed to call the emergency services and went to use my mobile phone.

At this point a man pointed out to me that if I used the orange emergency phone it would get through quicker and the operator would be able to locate exactly where the accident was. I asked him if he would call the emergency services on the orange phone, as he appeared to know exactly what he was doing. I noticed a lady sat on the embankment next to the hard shoulder crying and she appeared to be a bit shocked.

I asked an onlooker if he would mind sitting with her and talking to her until the ambulance got there. I thought this was important so that she felt supported and not alone.

Once that was done, the remaining onlookers and I decided to work as a team to remove the debris lying in the road, which would hinder the route for the oncoming emergency service vehicles."

Top tip

- Provide a response that is both concise and flows in a logical sequence.

PART 4 – How was it decided which way things were to be done?

"I decided to take the initiative and get everyone working as a team. I asked the people to let me know what their particular strengths were. One person was first aid trained and so he had the task of attending to the injured. Everyone agreed that we needed to work together as a team in order to achieve the task."

PART 5 – What did you do to ensure the team were able to get the result they wanted?

"I took control of a deteriorating situation and got everybody who was stood around doing nothing involved. I made sure I asked if anybody was skilled in certain areas such as first aid and used the people who had experience, such as the man who knew about the orange emergency telephones. I also kept talking to everybody and asking them if they were OK and happy with what they were doing. I tried my best to co-ordinate the people with jobs that I felt needed to be done as a priority."

Top tip

- Try to include details that demonstrate how your actions had a positive impact on the result.

PART 6 – What benefit did you see for yourself in what you did?

"The benefit overall was for the injured people, ensuring that they received treatment as soon as possible. However, I did feel a sense of achievement that the team had worked well together even though we had never met each other before. I also learnt a tremendous amount from the experience.

At the end we all shook hands and talked briefly and there was a common sense of achievement amongst everybody that we had done something positive. Without each other we wouldn't have been able to get the job done."

Top tip

- Try to explain that the benefit was positive.

QUESTIONS BASED AROUND YOUR REASONS AND MOTIVATIONS FOR WANTING TO BECOME A POLICE OFFICER

In addition to the standard core competency based questions, you may be asked additional questions that are centred around your motivations for wanting to become a police officer with this particular Police Service.

On the following pages we have provided a number of different questions and sample responses to assist you. Please remember that the responses provided here, and in other parts of this guide, are for guidance purposes only. The responses you provide on your application form must be based around your own individual circumstances, beliefs and circumstances.

SAMPLE QUESTION NUMBER 1

Q. How long have you been thinking about becoming a police officer and what has attracted your attention to the role?

Sample Response

"I have been considering a career as a police officer ever since I started my current sales manager job approximately 7 years ago. I enjoy working in a customer focused environment and thrive on providing high levels of service to customers. I have always been aware that the police officer's role is demanding, hard work and highly challenging but the rewards of such a job are what attracted my attention in the first place. The opportunity to work as part of an efficient team and work towards providing the community with an effective service would be highly rewarding and satisfying."

Top tips

- It is not advisable to state that you have only become interested recently. Candidates who have been seriously thinking about the job for a while will potentially score higher marks.

- Try to demonstrate in your response that you have studied the role carefully and that you believe your skills are suited to being a police officer.

- Those candidates who state that they are attracted solely to the 'catching criminals' side of the role will not score high.

- Read the core competencies and the job description carefully before responding to this question.

- Never be critical of a previous employer.

SAMPLE QUESTION NUMBER 2

Q. What have you done to prepare for this application?

Sample Response

"I have carried out a great deal of research to ascertain whether I am suitable for the role of a police officer and also to find out whether this career would suit my career aspirations. I have studied in-depth the police officer core competencies to ensure that I can meet the expectations of this Police Service. I have also carried out extensive research before applying to this particular Police Service as opposed to just applying to any constabulary and hoping that I just get in.

My research began on the Internet through the official police service websites, before finally studying this particular constabulary's website. I have also spoken to current serving police officers at my local station to ask about the role of a working police officer and how it affects their social life. Finally, I have discussed my intentions with my immediate family to ensure that I have their full support and encouragement."

Top tip

- You will recall at the beginning of this guide how much emphasis we placed on preparation leading to success. The police want to know how much preparation you have done and also the type of preparation. If you have carried out plenty of in-depth and meaningful preparation then it demonstrates to them that you are very serious about wanting this job. Those applicants who carry out little or no preparation may be simply 'going through the motions'.

Situational Judgement Questions

As we've mentioned, different forces use different types of application form. Instead of competency based or motivational questions, you might be asked to take a situational judgement test. A situational judgement test is a short assessment, which presents you with a number of short passages. You are then asked to rank the answers below the passage, based on their level of appropriateness. The situations that you'll encounter in the assessment are police-based. When answering situational judgement there is technically no right or wrong answer – the assessors want to see how you would react in that situation. However, there are certain responses which will make you less favourable with the assessors. For example, if you select 'punch your colleague' as efficient, then this could raise some red flags for the assessors!

The questions are usually presented in the same format. You are required to read a short passage, and will then be presented with four options. It is your job to separate the options into the following categories:

⇒ **EFFICIENT.** The most reliable, productive response, which is most likely to lead to a good result.

⇒ **FAIRLY EFFICIENT.** A reliable and productive response, albeit one which could possibly be improved upon, via small changes in action.

⇒ **INEFFICIENT.** A response which does not resolve or simply ignores the issue at hand.

⇒ **COUNTERPRODUCTIVE.** A response which makes the situation worse, rather than better.

Although the police situational judgement test is not perfect, it is generally a very reliable indicator of how an officer would act in a particular situation. Of course, it's very difficult to replicate potentially high-pressured situations in test format. However, the assessment is taken under timed conditions, which adds its own element of pressure for you to overcome.

Sample Police Situational Judgement Question

The following is a sample PSJT question for you to try. Following the question is a breakdown of how the answer has been reached.

Sample question

You are sitting in the staff canteen, when three other members of the constabulary sit down at your table. As you engage in friendly discussion with them, two of the members begin to mock the other person for his religion. Although they are only joking, you can see that the individual in question has been upset by these comments.

1. Join in, it's just a bit of banter.

Efficient / Fairly Efficient / Inefficient / Counterproductive

2. Speak up, and inform your colleagues that they should have more respect for other religions.

Efficient / Fairly Efficient / Inefficient / Counterproductive

3. Ask the offended colleague to speak to you in private afterwards, where you will discuss the comments.

Efficient / Fairly Efficient / Inefficient / Counterproductive

4. Try to change the subject.

Efficient / Fairly Efficient / Inefficient / Counterproductive

How to tackle the question

Whenever you are answering this type of police situational judgment question, **always try to focus your answer around the core competencies** of the police, whilst remaining true to what you would actually do in that situation.

'Join in, it's just a bit of banter.'

Answer: Counterproductive

Explanation: This is a counterproductive response. Religion is not something that should be mocked, and you can clearly see that the individual in question has taken the remarks badly.

'Speak up, and inform your colleagues that they should have more respect for other religions.'

Answer: Efficient

Explanation: This is an efficient response, as you are clearly demonstrating to the affected individual that discrimination of any kind will not be tolerated, as well as admonishing your colleagues for their behaviour.

'Ask the offended colleague to speak to you in private afterwards, where you will discuss the comments.'

Answer: Fairly Efficient

Explanation: This response is fairly efficient. You are showing your colleague that discrimination is not acceptable, but at the same time you are not demonstrating this to the individuals who have upset him.

'Try to change the subject.'

Answer: Inefficient

Explanation: This is an inefficient response. You need to make sure that the problem is addressed.

Tips for passing the Situational Judgement Test

There are several things you can do in order to help improve your scores during the PSJT. The following tips will help you to prepare effectively and improve your overall ability to pass this type of psychometric test:

TIP 1 – There are many types of Situational Judgement Tests available on the market. Just because you are applying to become a police officer, doesn't mean you should focus solely on police officer related SJTs. Obtain as many SJT questions as possible, from a variety of different genres, and practise accordingly.

TIP 2 – When you read the question, you will be presented with a 'situation'. Read the situation quickly before scanning each of the presented options. Look for the safest option first, and then look for the option you would be least likely to carry out. Then, assess the final two options and place them in order of priority based on what you would do in that type of situation.

TIP 3 – You do not need to be a police officer in order to pass the police officer related situational judgement test questions. What you do need to be is professionally conscious, and have a good level of common sense. When assessing the situation and presented options, always err on the side of caution. Don't take silly risks.

TIP 4 – Be entirely honest in how you answer the questions. This is very important. The role of a police officer involves a high degree of trust, integrity, professionalism, safety and a strict adherence to rules and procedures. The test is designed to assess how you would perform or react to given situations. You should also be aware that the police constabulary may ask you questions during the interview based on the answers you provide during the Situational Judgement Test. For example, if you answer a question during the PSJT that indicates you prefer to work alone as opposed to working as part of a team, yet you contradict yourself during one of the interview questions and state that you prefer to work as part of a team, this could lose you marks and imply you are dishonest. By answering the questions honestly during the test, you will not have to worry about how you answer the questions during the interview.

TIP 5 – Preparation is key! In the weeks leading up to your test, work hard to improve your skills in the testing areas. In addition to the tests contained within this guide there are numerous other testing resources available at www.How2Become.com. Try out as many test questions as possible and make sure you learn from your mistakes.

Now, have a go at the following practice questions. Check your answers against our ones afterwards!

Please note: none of the following questions or scenarios relate to actual events. The questions, scenarios and provided answers are completely fictitious. These questions are designed purely to provide preparation for those taking a situational judgement test. They are not representative of real questions or scenarios, nor are any laws, statements or suggested answers based on real life facts.

You can assist your preparation by reading the police code of ethics document, located on the College of Policing website. However, as an aspiring police officer, when undertaking the police situational judgement test you will most likely not be required to understand any laws or methods of policing. You should always answer the questions truthfully.

We recommend you try to answer these questions under timed conditions of no longer than 15 minutes!

Q1.

You are policing a local shopping centre. As you are walking past a clothing shop on the top floor, a man comes running past you at full speed. He knocks into you and falls to the ground. As he falls, he drops the bag in his hand, and a t-shirt falls out. You notice that the t-shirt still has the magnetic store tag on it.

Man: *'Sorry mate, didn't see you there! Must dash!'*

---

1. Help the man to his feet, put the t-shirt back in his bag for him and wish him a good day.

Efficient / Fairly Efficient / Inefficient / Counterproductive

2. Help the man to his feet, but examine the t-shirt, before questioning the man on where he got it from.

Efficient / Fairly Efficient / Inefficient / Counterproductive

3. Ask the man to come with you to the security office, so that you can investigate further. Explain to him that this is a precautionary step.

Efficient / Fairly Efficient / Inefficient / Counterproductive

4. Pin the man to the floor and proceed to arrest him.

Efficient / Fairly Efficient / Inefficient / Counterproductive

Q2.

> You are taking your lunch break at police HQ. As you sit down in the canteen, one of your colleagues approaches you. He sits down at your table and proceeds to inform you that he is a homosexual, and that you are the first person he has told.
>
> **Man:** *'Please try to keep this a secret, I'm scared of how I'll be treated if other people find out.'*

1. Inform your colleague that you have the utmost respect for him, regardless of his sexual preferences, and that his secret is safe with you.

Efficient / Fairly Efficient / Inefficient / Counterproductive

2. Inform your colleague that there is no reason to be ashamed of this, and encourage him to tell other people at the station.

Efficient / Fairly Efficient / Inefficient / Counterproductive

3. Inform your colleague that there is no place for people like him in the police force, and that he should hand in his badge.

Efficient / Fairly Efficient / Inefficient / Counterproductive

4. Inform your colleague that his secret is safe with you, before changing the topic of conversation.

Efficient / Fairly Efficient / Inefficient / Counterproductive

Q3.

You are the senior officer at a local police HQ. One day, one of your staff members knocks on your door. After inviting her in, she tells you the following:

Staff member: *'I'm really sorry sir, but I've made a mistake. While sorting through my paperwork, I accidentally shredded some of the key case reports on the Michelle Anthony murder investigation.'*

---

1. 'It's okay, we'll just have to proceed without those documents for now. Hopefully they won't be too important.'

Efficient / Fairly Efficient / Inefficient / Counterproductive

2. 'This is a disaster. You've derailed the entire investigation. I'm afraid you're sacked.'

Efficient / Fairly Efficient / Inefficient / Counterproductive

3. 'Okay, don't panic. I'll contact the senior administrator, who should have photocopies of the forms. Later this afternoon though we'll have a serious chat about this.'

Efficient / Fairly Efficient / Inefficient / Counterproductive

4. 'Can you explain to me how this happened? This is a very serious incident.'

Efficient / Fairly Efficient / Inefficient / Counterproductive

Q4.

> You are on duty with a fellow officer, at your local shopping centre. The two of you are in the middle of patrolling the top floor, when you pass by a particular clothing shop. Your fellow officer gets very excited, dashes into the shop and starts trying on denim jackets.
>
> **Fellow officer:** *'I love this shop! I might have to buy a few things from here!'*

1. Inform your fellow officer that they are acting very unprofessionally, and tell them to get back to work.

   Efficient / Fairly Efficient / Inefficient / Counterproductive

2. Leave your fellow officer to it. It's not your problem if they want to mess around.

   Efficient / Fairly Efficient / Inefficient / Counterproductive

3. Inform your fellow officer that you'll be reporting them to your head of station for this.

   Efficient / Fairly Efficient / Inefficient / Counterproductive

4. Laugh. They are only having a bit of fun.

   Efficient / Fairly Efficient / Inefficient / Counterproductive

Q5.

You are on duty by yourself, walking through a residential area. Your partner has been taken ill, and you are due to receive a new partner shortly. As you walk through the area, you see a man on a ladder, climbing in through the upstairs window of a house. There are no cars parked on the driveway.

1. Ignore it. He's probably just forgotten his keys.

Efficient / Fairly Efficient / Inefficient / Counterproductive

2. Immediately call the station to ask for backup. You may need help to apprehend the criminal.

Efficient / Fairly Efficient / Inefficient / Counterproductive

3. Wait for the man to exit the property, and then confront him.

Efficient / Fairly Efficient / Inefficient / Counterproductive

4. Immediately attempt to enter the property yourself. You need to stop the man before he gets away.

Efficient / Fairly Efficient / Inefficient / Counterproductive

Q6.

> Overnight, the local park has been declared as a crime scene. You have been tasked with ensuring that nobody enters the park, which has been cordoned off with crime scene tape. All of a sudden, a man approaches you:
>
> **Man:** *'Hi there, I left my bag in the park yesterday afternoon. It should be on the bench near the water fountain. Is it okay if I go in and get it? I'll only be 2 minutes.'*

1. 'I'll have to ask my senior officer about that, give me a moment.'

Efficient / Fairly Efficient / Inefficient / Counterproductive

2. 'Sure, go right ahead, just tell them that I let you in.'

Efficient / Fairly Efficient / Inefficient / Counterproductive

3. 'I'm sorry sir but this is a crime scene, we can't allow anyone to enter.'

Efficient / Fairly Efficient / Inefficient / Counterproductive

4. 'Since your bag has been left at the scene, it could be used as evidence. For this reason, I'm afraid I can't retrieve it for you.'

Efficient / Fairly Efficient / Inefficient / Counterproductive

Q7.

You are working at police HQ. You have a mountain of paperwork to get through, when your senior officer approaches you.

Senior Officer: *'Hey, I need you to fill in this form urgently, it's in regard to the Conningway case. Can you get it back to me in the next hour?'*

1. 'If you say please.'

Efficient / Fairly Efficient / Inefficient / Counterproductive

2. 'I'll do my best, although I've got a lot of paperwork to complete. Would you prefer me to prioritise this form?'

Efficient / Fairly Efficient / Inefficient / Counterproductive

3. 'No chance, you'll have to wait until tomorrow.'

Efficient / Fairly Efficient / Inefficient / Counterproductive

4. 'Sure, I'll give it immediate priority.'

Efficient / Fairly Efficient / Inefficient / Counterproductive

Q8.

You are on evening patrol with another officer. As you pass the local pub, a man staggers outside. He is bleeding from the nose. Another man follows him out and knocks him to the floor with a punch. The two begin to scuffle on the ground.

Fellow officer: *'Oh dear. Let's call for backup, there's no point in endangering ourselves by getting involved.'*

1. Inform your fellow officer that it's your duty to protect the public, and immediately intervene.

Efficient / Fairly Efficient / Inefficient / Counterproductive

2. Allow your fellow officer to call for backup, while trying to intervene yourself.

Efficient / Fairly Efficient / Inefficient / Counterproductive

3. Agree with your fellow officer. There's no point putting yourself in danger.

Efficient / Fairly Efficient / Inefficient / Counterproductive

4. Encourage your fellow officer to intervene, while you call for backup.

Efficient / Fairly Efficient / Inefficient / Counterproductive

Q9.

The day is Thursday. You've been working with your current partner for just under a month now, but have noticed that this person keeps clocking out from your shifts early. As you approach the end of the day, he says:

'Right, I'm off now. See you tomorrow.'

The time is 16:30, and he's due to finish at 17:00.

---

1. 'Alright, bye.'

Efficient / Fairly Efficient / Inefficient / Counterproductive

2. 'You've finished early a few times recently. Your shift isn't meant to end till 5pm.'

Efficient / Fairly Efficient / Inefficient / Counterproductive

3. 'I'm going to tell police HQ about this.'

Efficient / Fairly Efficient / Inefficient / Counterproductive

4. 'Our shift doesn't finish for another half an hour. Get back here, or else…'

Efficient / Fairly Efficient / Inefficient / Counterproductive

Q10.

> You are on your lunchbreak, and stop by a local newsagent. As you walk through the store, you notice a young man with a bag of sweets under his arm leaving the shop. The man doesn't seem to have visited the till, but the alarm isn't going off.

1. Approach the shopkeeper and inform him that you believe someone has just stolen from his store.

Efficient / Fairly Efficient / Inefficient / Counterproductive

2. Ignore the situation. The man has probably paid.

Efficient / Fairly Efficient / Inefficient / Counterproductive

3. Follow the man out of the shop and question him.

Efficient / Fairly Efficient / Inefficient / Counterproductive

4. Ask the shopkeeper if you can take a look at the shop's CCTV footage.

Efficient / Fairly Efficient / Inefficient / Counterproductive

Answers to Situational Judgement Questions.

Q1.

1. Help the man to his feet, put the t-shirt back in his bag for him and wish him a good day.

Answer: Inefficient

Explanation: The reason that this answer is inefficient, is that you are not resolving the issue. Instead, you are simply ignoring it and letting the man leave.

2. Help the man to his feet, but examine the t-shirt, before questioning the man on where he got it from.

Answer: Fairly Efficient

Explanation: The reason that is answer is fairly efficient, is that you are taking steps to deal with the problem. However, there is every chance that the man won't tell you the truth, so simply questioning him doesn't give you the chance to investigate entirely.

3. Ask the man to come with you to the security office, so that you can investigate further. Explain to him that this is a precautionary step.

Answer: Efficient

Explanation: The reason that this answer is efficient, is that you are taking all of the necessary steps to resolve the issue, including explaining to the man why you have taken this course of action.

4. Pin the man to the floor and proceed to arrest him.

Answer: Counterproductive

Explanation: The reason that this is counterproductive is because you are immediately jumping to (aggressive) conclusions about the man's behaviour. It could well be a mistake. Pinning him to the floor should be a last resort, when all other potential avenues have been exhausted.

Q2.

1. Inform your colleague that you have the utmost respect for him, regardless of his sexual preferences, and that his secret is safe with you.

Answer: Efficient

Explanation: The reason that this answer is efficient is because you are showing your colleague respect/demonstrating a good level of tolerance, and helping him to gain trust in you by assuring him that the information will remain confidential.

2. Inform your colleague that there is no reason to be ashamed of this, and encourage him to tell other people at the station.

Answer: Inefficient.

Explanation: This is inefficient, as you are encouraging the individual to go around telling other people at the station, when this is not a matter that needs to be discussed. Whatever the man's sexual preferences, this is not an appropriate topic of conversation in the workplace, and is only acceptable in this circumstance because he has confided in you. Casually discussing the issue with everyone else at the station is unnecessary.

3. Inform your colleague that there is no place for people like him in the police force, and that he should hand in his badge.

Answer: Counterproductive

Explanation: This is counterproductive, because you are showing extreme intolerance, and making the individual feel unwelcome. Also, the statement that you are making is completely untrue.

4. Inform your colleague that his secret is safe with you, before changing the topic of conversation.

Answer: Fairly Efficient

Explanation: This is fairly efficient because you are assuring your colleague of your confidentiality, and then changing the conversation onto something more appropriate for the workplace environment.

Q3.

1. 'It's okay, we'll just have to proceed without those documents for now. Hopefully they won't be too important.'

Answer: Inefficient

Explanation: The reason that this answer is inefficient is because the documents are important, and that it's likely you will need them later down the line. In this answer, you are simply ignoring the problem.

2. 'This is a disaster. You've derailed the entire investigation. I'm afraid you're sacked.'

Answer: Counterproductive

Explanation: The reason that this is counterproductive is because in this answer, you are taking extremely rash and unnecessary action. Furthermore, based on the role that this question gives you (senior officer) there is no indication that you have the power to remove people from their job.

3. 'Okay, don't panic. I'll contact the senior administrator, who should have photocopies of the forms. Later this afternoon though we'll have a serious chat about this.'

Answer: Efficient

Explanation: The reason that this response is efficient, is because you are offering a solution to the problem, calming the individual down, and informing them that there could be repercussions for their mistake.

4. 'Can you explain to me how this happened? This is a very serious incident.'

Answer: Fairly Efficient

Explanation: The reason that this response is fairly efficient, is because you are taking a serious approach to this problem, and identifying to the individual that it needs to be dealt with.

Q4.

1. Inform your fellow officer that they are acting very unprofessionally, and tell them to get back to work.

Answer: Efficient

Explanation: This is the most efficient response. You are clearly indicating to your partner that they are not acting in an acceptable manner, and are encouraging them to focus on the job at hand – policing.

2. Leave your fellow officer to it. It's not your problem if they want to mess around.

Answer: Inefficient

Explanation: This is inefficient, as you are simply ignoring the issue.

3. Inform your fellow officer that you'll be reporting them to your head of station for this.

Answer: Fairly Efficient

Explanation: This is fairly efficient, albeit perhaps a little unnecessary. In this instance, your colleague's unprofessional behaviour could be dealt with by giving them a stern warning, rather than immediately escalating the matter to the head of station.

4. Laugh. They are only having a bit of fun.

Answer: Counterproductive.

Explanation: This is counterproductive. By laughing, you are encouraging their behaviour.

Q5.

1. Ignore it. He's probably just forgotten his keys.

Answer: Inefficient

Explanation: The reason that this is inefficient, is because you aren't doing anything to act upon a potentially serious situation. At the very least, you need to question the man.

2. Immediately call the station to ask for backup. You may need help to apprehend the criminal.

Answer: Fairly Efficient

Explanation: This is a fairly efficient response, as you are taking steps to secure your own safety, and to deal with the problem. That being said, it's entirely possible that this is just a misunderstanding, and in any case your new partner is due to arrive shortly.

3. Wait for the man to exit the property, and then confront him.

Answer: Efficient

Explanation: This is an efficient response. Instead of going charging in, assuming the worst, wait for the man to exit the property. This means that you can deal with him in a calm and professional manner.

4. Immediately attempt to enter the property yourself. You need to stop the man before he gets away.

Answer: Counterproductive

Explanation: This is a rash and potentially damaging decision, especially if the person turns out to be the homeowner/has just forgotten their keys. Furthermore, in attempting to enter the property yourself (by force) you will probably end up damaging the house.

Q6.

1. 'I'll have to ask my senior officer about that, give me a moment.'

Answer: Inefficient

Explanation: This is inefficient, as you already know that members of the public are not allowed inside the perimeter. Therefore, you would be wasting the time of both yourself and your senior officer by asking him.

2. 'Sure, go right ahead, just tell them that I let you in.'

Answer: Counterproductive

Explanation: This is counterproductive, as you are completely breaking the rules. It's a crime scene, meaning the public cannot enter.

3. 'I'm sorry sir but this is a crime scene, we can't allow anyone to enter.'

Answer: Efficient

Explanation: This is a crime scene, meaning that members of the public are absolutely not allowed in. The most efficient response is to politely but firmly deny the man entrance.

4. 'Since your bag has been left at the scene, it could be used as evidence. For this reason, I'm afraid I can't retrieve it for you.'

Answer: Fairly Efficient

Explanation: This is a fairly efficient response, as it tells the person why they cannot have their bag back. However, it does not explain that members of the public are not allowed on the crime scene.

Q7.

1. 'If you say please.'

Answer: Counterproductive

Explanation: This is rude/disrespectful to your superior.

2. 'I'll do my best, although I've got a lot of paperwork to complete. Would you prefer me to prioritise this form?'

Answer: Efficient

Explanation: This is efficient, as you are assuring the officer that you will do your best to complete the task, whilst also giving them an explanation for why it might be difficult.

3. 'No chance, you'll have to wait until tomorrow.'

Answer: Inefficient

Explanation: Not only is this quite rude, but you are giving no attempt or effort to try and get the work completed, nor are you even providing an explanation.

4. 'Sure, I'll give it immediate priority.'

Answer: Fairly Efficient

Explanation: This is a fairly efficient response, although it does not take into account the other work that you need to do.

Q8.

1. Inform your fellow officer that it's your duty to protect the public, and immediately intervene.

Answer: Efficient

Explanation: As a police officer, you have a duty of care for the public. You need to step in and stop this fight from escalating even further.

2. Allow your fellow officer to call for backup, while trying to intervene yourself.

Answer: Fairly Efficient

Explanation: This is fairly efficient, as at least you are intervening in the fight. However, something of this nature should really not require more than two of you (unless things seriously escalate) and therefore it's better if your partner assists you in intervening.

3. Agree with your fellow officer. There's no point putting yourself in danger.

Answer: Counterproductive

Explanation: As a police officer, you have a duty of care to the public. By refusing to intervene, you are neglecting this duty.

4. Encourage your fellow officer to intervene, while you call for backup.

Answer: Inefficient

Explanation: Although this is technically the same as option 2, encouraging your partner to intervene whilst you make the call to the station is not particularly bold on your part; particularly as your partner believes that you should ignore the fight altogether.

Q9.

1. 'Alright, bye.'

Answer: Inefficient.

Explanation: This is inefficient, as you are simply allowing your partner to leave, without resolving the issue.

2. 'You've finished early a few times recently. Your shift isn't meant to end till 5pm.'

Answer: Efficient

Explanation: This is an efficient response, as you are calling your partner out on his questionable behaviour.

3. 'I'm going to tell police HQ about this.'

Answer: Fairly Efficient

Explanation: This is fairly efficient, as you are making an effort to resolve the situation. However, it's entirely possible that your partner hasn't realised they've been finishing early, so it's worth discussing with them first, before going to police HQ about the issue.'

4. 'Our shift doesn't finish for another half an hour. Get back here, or else…'

Answer: Counterproductive

Explanation: This is counterproductive. The use of the phrase 'or else' implies a threat, making this unacceptable behaviour.

Q10.

1. Approach the shopkeeper and inform him that you believe someone has just stolen from his store.

Answer: Efficient

Explanation: This is an efficient response. The shopkeeper can confirm whether or not the individual has paid. If he hasn't, you should then have time to apprehend him.

2. Ignore the situation. The man has probably paid.

Answer: Counterproductive

Explanation: This is counterproductive, as you are simply ignoring the issue.

3. Follow the man out of the shop and question him.

Answer: Fairly Efficient

Explanation: This is a fairly efficient response. You are taking direct action to deal with the problem. However, it's better to approach the shopkeeper first, before assuming the worst about the individual.

4. Ask the shopkeeper if you can take a look at the shop's CCTV footage.

Answer: Inefficient

Explanation: This is an inefficient response. There are no grounds for you to look at the CCTV footage, especially not before ascertaining whether the man has stolen.

The New Police Assessment Centre

If you pass the application stage, then you will be invited to attend an assessment centre, at a location which will be revealed to you by the police (such as the Metropolitan's HQ building – the Empress State Building). This is known as the Day One assessment centre.

When you find out the venue and time at which the assessment centre will be held, take the time to learn exactly where this is and how long it will take to get there – taking traffic into account. You do NOT want to be caught out and arrive late to the assessment centre, as this will look extremely unprofessional and severely hinder your chances of progression.

The assessment centre is usually conducted over a period of five hours. You will take part in the assessment centre along with a large group of other candidates who have made it this far. There will normally be various opportunities for breaks, where candidates can have something to eat or drink, however this is not a guarantee – so it's recommended that you try and eat before the assessment day if possible.

When you are invited to attend the assessment centre, you'll be asked to bring a number of important documents with you to confirm your identification to the police. The forms of identification can vary but the more common types include:

- A full 10-year passport or TWO of the following:
- British Driving Licence;
- P45;
- Birth Certificate, issued within six weeks of birth;
- Cheque Book and Bank Card with three statements and proof of signature;
- Card containing a photograph of yourself;
- Proof of residence, e.g. Council Tax, Gas, Electricity, Water or Telephone Bill.

Make sure that you read the information given to you and take along the relevant documents as if you do not, then you won't be able to continue with the day.

What's New?

The new assessment centre is extremely different to the old one. For a start, the new centre has a much friendlier atmosphere. During previous national assessment days, you were basically just a number in a system, and were processed by staff in conveyor belt fashion. There were no attempts to greet you or get to know you. At the new assessment day, staff will shake your hand and welcome you warmly to the centre.

On top of this, the assessments have very much changed. Whereas before you were placed in the role of a customer services officer – now the police have created assessments where you are an acting police officer or constable. The reason behind this is that they want to challenge candidates on their potential policing skills, before they get the job. Just like before though, the assessment centre still focuses heavily on the competencies and values.

When you arrive at the centre, the first thing that will happen is that you'll be given a lanyard – containing your name and a number, and an iPad. That's right, the new police assessment centre will be using iPads – with some of the focus being around how quickly you can adapt to new forms of technology. In every single assessment, you'll need to use your iPad in some way, shape or form. The number on your lanyard will be used to log you into your iPad. You'll also be provided with a keyboard, which you can use to write notes or text on the iPad. All candidates to the assessment centre will be provided with strict instructions not to skip ahead on their iPads, as they must stay on track with the exercise they are currently taking. Don't worry, the police will brief you on how to use an iPad at the start of the day. However, it's definitely worth getting hold of one in advance if you can, just so you can familiarise yourself with how it works.

BONUS TIP: you will undertake a few written tasks at the assessment centre where you will use a keyboard connected to your iPad. Get practice in now to make sure you are comfortable typing quickly and efficiently on a keyboard.

Due to the number of people taking the assessment centre, candidates will be broken up into groups. Generally, they'll try and make the groups as even as possible (for example 5 groups of 5). Each group of people will then be asked to take a different assessment. So, this means that there is no set order for which assessments you'll take, it very much depends on what group you're in. To make things clearer for you, the police will provide you with a laminated schedule when you arrive, which shows exactly what assessments you'll be taking and when.

The Tests

So, what about the new tests? While there's still some elements of the old assessment centre that remain, these elements have changed, and there's also some brand-new exercises too. There are five parts to the new assessment centre, with 7 tests to take in total. These are as follows:

- Role play exercises. You will take two role play exercises, one involving one role play actor and another exercise involving two role play actors.

- A virtual reality exercise.

- An interactive video task. You will take two video exercises, one focusing on observation and one focusing on situational judgement and observation.

- A written exercise.

- An interview.

Prior to each test, you will be told how long the exercise will take, and how preparation time will be afforded.

Now, let's look at all of these exercises in a bit more detail.

Role Play

Role play is a form of interactive exercise. Essentially, you are given a brief of a scenario, and then 5 minutes to prepare. You will then walk into a room containing one or two actors, and then required to play the role of a police constable, to deal with their situation. During the briefing period, you will be able to use your iPad to make notes. You'll be allowed to bring these notes into the room with you. The briefing will be delivered to you on your iPad, so you'll need to read through the information using this device.

There are two role play scenarios in total at the new police assessment centre, and each of them will last for 10 minutes, with 5 minutes briefing for each. During the first role play exercise you will need to deal with one role play actor. During the second role play exercise there will be two actors, for whom you will need to resolve a dispute.

iPad usage aside, the above is highly similar to how the police role play has always been (minus the two actors). However, here's where things get different:

First of all, in line with creating a 'friendlier' atmosphere, you will now get to meet the assessor prior to taking the role play exercise. This was not the case before, where you entered the room and the assessor just sat in the corner, silently marking you. Now, the assessor will greet you at the door, introduce themselves and ask you to enter the room once you're ready.

The scenarios are different now too. Whereas before you would be placed in the role of a customer services officer, now (as mentioned) you are a police constable, responding to a situation. Obviously, we can't give you the definitive scenario that you'll face, but here are some things which are likely to come up:

- Resolving a dispute between neighbours, co-workers or other members of the public.

- Dealing with a member of the public who is behaving in an aggressive or threatening manner.

- Encouraging a young or vulnerable person to amend their behaviour.

The role plays are designed to be much more reflective of real life now. The actors will not hesitate to give you definitive opinions and views, which is not something they would do in the previous assessment centre. For example, if you asked the actor in the previous assessment centre whether they've found your advice helpful/it resolves their problem, they might give you a vague response. Now, the actor will say words to the effect of 'No that didn't help, you're useless!' or 'Yes, you've been of great help'. If the former, then you'll be expected to come up with alternative solutions or ways of resolving the problem, or at the very least exploring why the actor feels that way.

In regards to the solutions that you come up with, you will be expected to use common sense to work around the problems. You will also be expected to demonstrate emotional awareness and persuasive techniques, to get the actor to cooperate with you. The assessor will also focus on elements such as body language – which is an important part of communication. You need to treat this situation as you would a real-life scenario.

When it comes to scoring on this assessment, the assessor will score you based on how well you have demonstrated the core competencies and values. You will be given a score from 1-5, with 5 being the highest, on each competency/value.

Now, let's look at some example exercises. Please note that the situations in these exercises are not a direct reflection on the scenarios you'll encounter at the police assessment centre. In these scenarios we have walked you through each stage of the exercise, to show you how to go about tackling it.

Let's start with preparation.

The Preparation Phase

As we have mentioned, you will be given 5 minutes preparation time for each exercise. The briefing will be delivered to you in the form of an email or a document on your iPad, along with any additional documentation that is relevant to the scenario. You'll usually be taken to a separate, quiet area before the assessment starts, so that you can make the most of this preparation time. It's extremely important that you use the preparation time wisely. 5 minutes is a very short amount of time, and this is part of the reason that it's so important to fully understand the competencies before you attend the assessment centre. You should immediately be able to look at the briefing notes and develop an idea of how you'll approach the situation, and which competencies you will use to do so. You should make a concerted attempt to learn as much about the role of a police officer as possible, so that you have a good idea of how to approach the scenario.

During the briefing, this is how we recommend you spend the time:

- First, quickly read the scenario and any supporting information/ documentation. If you have already studied the welcome pack prior to assessment your life will be a lot easier.

- Once you have studied the scenario and any additional information/documentation you should then separate relevant information from irrelevant information. Write down brief notes as to what you think is relevant.

- You now need to cross match any relevant information from the scenario with procedures, policies and your responsibilities that are provided in the Welcome Pack. For example, if within the scenario it becomes apparent that somebody is being bullied or harassed, you will need to know, use and make reference to the police values during the scenario.

- Finally, we recommend that you write down on your iPad a step by step approach on what you intend to do during the activity stage. An example of this may be as follows:

STEP 1

Introduce yourself to the role actor and ask him/her how you can help them. Remember to be polite and respectful and treat the role play actor in a sensitive and supportive manner.

STEP 2

Listen to them carefully and ask relevant questions to establish the facts. (How, When, Where, Why, Who)

STEP 3

Clarify the information received to check you have understood exactly what has happened.

STEP 4

Provide a suitable solution to the problem or situation and tell the role play actor what you intend to do. (Remember to use keywords and phrases from the core competencies).

STEP 5

Check to confirm that the role play actor is happy with your solution. Provide a final summary of what you intend to do and ask them if there is anything else you can help them with.

(Tell the role actor that you will take responsibility for solving the problem and that you will keep them updated on progress)

Obviously, the above really depends on the situation. As we've mentioned, there could be multiple role play actors in the room for you, and it might even be the case that you have to resolve a dispute between both of them, or calm them down, before you can come up with an actual solution.

Once you have made your notes and created a plan of action you are now ready to go through to the activity phase. Before we move on to this stage of the role play assessment we will provide you with a further explanation of how you may wish to approach the preparation phase using a sample scenario.

SAMPLE ROLE PLAY EXERCISE 1

You have been called out to deal with an inc
mums outside a school. The two women are bickering
and threatening to hurt one another. One of the women mak
racial comment towards the other.

How to Prepare

If you have already taken the time to study the police values prior to attending the assessment, then two things should immediately jump out at you: the threats, and the discrimination. Neither of these are acceptable. Remember that both the police values and the core competencies specifically address behaviour of this kind, and it is a requirement for police officers to identify and challenge this.

Using the 5-step plan, the following is how you might deal with this type of situation:

STEP 1 – Walk into the activity room and introduce yourself to the role actors. You should immediately challenge the language that was used, and inform them that this is completely unacceptable. Ask them sensitively what the problem is and how you can help them. If there is a chair(s) available in the room then ask them to sit down. If the two women continue to argue, then you will need to take steps to calm them down, using persuasive and authoritative language and techniques.

STEP 2 – Listen very carefully to both sides of the argument. Give each person equal opportunity to speak and say their part, and sympathise where appropriate. You can then start to establish facts, asking each person relevant questions about their side of the story, such as:

- Why do they feel the other person is in the wrong?

- What would they like to be done to resolve the situation?

- Was there anyone else involved in this incident?

STEP 3 – Clarify and confirm with the two actors that you have gathered all of the correct information and facts.

STEP 4 – At this stage you need to tell the actors about exactly how you intend to deal with the situation. Make specific reference to the police values and core competencies, and use this as the basis for resolving the issue.

STEP 5 – Finally, you need to make sure that both actors are happy with your intended solution. Obviously, since there are two actors, it might be difficult to completely appease both parties 100%. Still, you should endeavour to do your best and find a reasonable and law-abiding solution. Provide them both with a final summary of what you intend to do and then ask them if there's anything else that you can help with. You should also confirm that you are happy to take responsibility for resolving the issue and that you will keep them updated on any progress as and when it occurs (assuming there's further problems to deal with).

Once the 5-minute preparation phase is complete, you will then move to the activity stage of the assessment.

The Activity Phase

The activity stage will again last for 5 minutes and it is during this phase that you are required to interact with the role actor or actors.

As mentioned, you'll be greeted at the door by the assessor, who will introduce themselves and ask you to give them a couple of seconds and then enter the room. As soon as you enter the room, the exercise will begin. The assessor will sit in the corner of the room, and will not speak whilst the exercise is happening. You should do your best to ignore them, and concentrate fully on engaging with the actor.

Below we have provided you with some sample responses and suggestions for how you might deal with this type of exercise, again using the example of two mums bickering outside the school gates. For the purposes of this exercise, the two mums are called Mrs Gibbs, and Mrs Earnshaw.

SAMPLE RESPONSES AND ACTIONS TO EXERCISE 1

Response

'Mrs Gibbs, Mrs Earnshaw, I would like you to come over here please. Thank you. First of all, I have been informed that threatening and racial behaviour has potentially taken place. Let me say that this behaviour and language is entirely unacceptable, in any way, shape or form. I am here to resolve your issue, but I will absolutely not tolerate any form of discrimination. Is this clear?'

Explanation

This is a good opening when dealing with this type of situation. You are being firm and authoritative, whilst addressing a key issue, and assuring the two women that you will resolve the issue. Remember to use open body language, and don't become confrontational, defensive or aggressive.

Top tip

- If you initially struggle to stop the actors bickering or to get your attention, try speaking clearer and louder. It's important that you can show you can take control of a situation, so it would be wise to practice using persuasive and authoritative language and techniques (but in no way threatening!) prior to your assessment day.

Response

'Thank you. Now, I would like to take the opportunity to get both sides of the story. I can assure you that both of you will get an equal opportunity to address the problem. So, Mrs Gibbs, could you please explain to me what the problem is, and how you would like us to address it.'

'Okay, thank you for explaining that. Now I'd like to ask a few questions, if that's okay, just so that I have a clearer idea of exactly what the main issue is here.'

'Okay, and how did that make you feel? What do you think could have been done differently?'

'I totally sympathise, I understand this must have been hard for you.'

'Now, Mrs Earnshaw, I would like to hear your side of the story. Please explain to me clearly about what you think the problem is, and how you would like us to address it.'

'Thank you for explaining that, Mrs Earnshaw. Just as I did with Mrs Gibbs, I'd now like to take the opportunity to ask you a few questions based on what you've told me.'

Explanation

This is a good follow up. You are clearly explaining the approach that you will take, to the two relevant parties, and making it clear that they will be treated equally and fairly. You are also giving them a chance to address what outcome they'd like to see from this issue. Asking questions shows interest and care for the customer, and will give them assurance that you are genuinely invested in resolving the problem for them.

Response

'Okay, thank you both for being patient. I would like to take the chance to clarify a few facts from what you have told me, just so that I am clear on everything. Is this okay?'

Explanation

This is a good way to approach the clarification stage. You are being reasonable and polite, whilst still clearly explaining to the relevant parties about exactly what you are doing. Again you are focusing on the needs of the people in question, which is important. Try to look and sound genuine and also use suitable facial expressions. In order to 'problem solve' you must first ask questions and gather the facts of the incident.

Response

'Thank you for being so patient. I have considered everything that both of you have said, and I would like to come to a compromise that works for both of you. Here is what I intend to do. *List your solution*. Obviously I understand that this is not a perfect solution, but I feel that this gives the best possible chance for both of you to walk away from this incident as happy as possible. Now that I have explained what I'm going to do, I'd like you both to tell me how you feel about this. Mrs Gibbs, does this solution work for you?'

'Okay, thank you, Mrs Gibbs. I am glad we have reached a solution to your problem. Mrs Earnshaw, does this solution work for you?'

'As I said, I understand this is not a perfect fix, but I hope you can recognise that I am doing my best to resolve the situation in a way that works for both of you. Please could you tell me what you don't like about my solution, Mrs Earnshaw, and we can see if this is resolvable.'

Explanation

Here you are being clear and decisive on the course of action that you are going to take, and showing a caring nature/high level of service. You are inviting the role play actors to give feedback on your intended solution, and giving them a chance to demonstrate whether this is a reasonable resolution to the issue. Where one of the role play actors is unhappy with your intended solution, you are taking steps to gage why this is the case, and making a concentrated attempt to put it right.

Now, let's have a look at another exercise.

⌐ ROLE PLAY EXERCISE 2

Y. .ave been called out to a local shopping centre. A teenage girl has been arrested for shoplifting. The security team are familiar with the girl, and have been dealing with bad behaviour from her for the past year. They believe that she's gone off the rails, and has started hanging out with the wrong type of people. The shopping centre do not want to press charges, but the head of the security team has asked you to have a word with the girl.

How to prepare

When reading the above, you need to take into account the following factors, which should have an impact on how you approach this situation:

- The centre do not want to press charges. This means that you don't need to go into the situation as if you were making an arrest.

- The centre have specifically asked you to have a word with the girl. This means that you need to demonstrate a high level of emotional awareness, understanding, and persuasive technique.

- This is not the first time the girl has been caught misbehaving at the shopping centre. On top of this, she's been caught shoplifting. So, you still need to take a firm approach.

Using the 5-step plan, the following is how you might deal with this type of situation:

STEP 1 – Walk into the activity room and introduce yourself to the role play actor. Take a friendly approach, whilst still emphasising the seriousness of the situation. You should start by challenging her over her behaviour. Even though you have been brought in to 'have a chat', it goes without saying that her actions are unacceptable, and therefore this needs to be made clear before anything else is said. Once you've discussed her actions, tell her that centre aren't pressing charges, but that you want to have a serious talk about her behaviour.

STEP 2 – Ask the actor questions about her behaviour in the past year, and try to determine whether she feels her behaviour is unacceptable. Try and focus on the positive aspects of the actor's character, not her weaknesses. You should aim to take an encouraging and compassionate approach.

STEP 3 – Ask the actor how she is feeling about what you've said, and her thoughts on her own behaviour. Ask the actor what she would like the next steps to be.

STEP 4 – Based on the actor's thoughts, try and suggest improvements to her course of action, or ideas and opinions on how you think she should proceed. This part will involve going back and forth with the actor on the benefits of different behavioural changes.

STEP 5 – Finally, you need to agree on a course of action. Clearly relate this action to the actor, and take steps to ensure that she has completely understood it. Make sure she is happy with the suggested ideas, and then take her details for further follow up later on.

Now, let's move onto the activity phase, and some sample responses. For the purposes of this exercise, let's assume that the teenage girl is named Claire.

SAMPLE RESPONSES AND ACTIONS TO EXERCISE 2

Response

'Hi Claire. I've been asked to come and speak to you today by the shopping centre. I'm aware there's been a very serious incident. I would like you to know that the shopping centre aren't intending to press charges, however this is still a very serious matter and therefore we need to discuss it. Do you understand how serious this incident is?'

'Shoplifting is really serious. It's against the law, and therefore you have committed a crime. My aim today isn't to punish you, I just want to find out why you did it and how we can work together to prevent this sort of thing from happening in the future.'

'I'm glad you understand. If it's okay with you, I'd like to have an in-depth chat about what's going on with you right now.'

Explanation

This is a great opening. You are setting out your stall early – making it very clear that this type of behaviour is unacceptable, whilst still underlining the main point of the meeting – which is to have a talk about the girl's behaviour and how it can be improved. In the above responses you have taken a compassionate approach, clearly giving Claire a say in how this meeting is conducted and establishing whether she is comfortable.

Response

'Okay, I'm glad we're on the same page. Let's talk about today's incident first. Can you explain to me why you did it? I mean, what thoughts and feelings did you have leading up to the incident?'

'I totally get that, and I know it might seem like a bit of fun to wind the centre staff up, but they have jobs to do to. I've spoken to the centre security and they are a bit worried about you. They said they've seen you hanging around outside smoking and are also concerned by the type of people you're associating with.'

'I get that, and I know they are your friends, but do you also understand that we are worried about you? Nobody would ever tell you who you can and can't be friends with, but it's my job and the job of the rest of the staff here to look out for your welfare.'

'You're not stupid at all. You're a very bright young girl, with a great future ahead of you. That's why we are worried, because nobody wants to see you throw it away.'

Explanation

Here, you are taking a compassionate and thoughtful approach, showing a great level of emotional awareness. You are showing Claire that you understand how she feels and making it clear that you have her best interests at heart. You are highlighting the positive aspects of her character, to make her feel self-confident and more aware of the harmful connotations of her behaviour.

Response

'I'm glad you see where I'm coming from. I really think that together we can make a positive change. I want to know how you feel though. Are things at home difficult, or has anything happened recently that's made you feel upset? What would you like to see change? What kind of things are you interested in/passionate about?'

Explanation

In this response you are giving Claire the chance to provide you with feedback and have a genuine say in how she can bring about positive change. This is a good way to introduce the 'change' element of this exercise, as it helps Claire to feel more in control and confident about having the chance to explain her thoughts and feelings. Likewise, you've also tried to engage with Claire on a personal level a bit more. This is a good approach to take with role play – engaging with someone's passion and interest builds up a sense of rapport, and means they'll be more likely to work with you rather than against you.

Response

'Okay, great, that's really positive! I think the ideas you've mentioned are really good, and some of them are really creative. I definitely think we can implement...'

'I will be happy to help you implement these and bring about a positive change.'

'If it's okay, I'd like to suggest a few small changes, just based on my own thoughts about this situation. '

Explanation

This is a great follow up. You are being really positive, and showing Claire that you appreciate her ideas and opinions. You are also using this as an opportunity to assess the changes and add your thoughts and views, whilst emphasising that you will be happy to play a key role in implementing the changes.

Response

'I'm really glad that we could agree on this course of action. Before you go, I just want to clarify that you are totally happy with everything that we've discussed and how we're going to implement it.'

'Okay, thank you. I really appreciate you taking the time to speak with me. If it's okay, I'd like to take some contact details, so I can call you later this week to follow up.'

'It was great speaking to you, and I'm glad we could resolve this amicably.'

Explanation

This is a great way to finish the conversation. You are leaving things on a really positive note, and ensuring that there's a way for you to follow up on the incident later on. You are also making sure that the actor totally understands the agreed course of action, and is happy with it.

The above role play scenario is designed to test your emotional awareness, community support, and also your persuasiveness. Again, learning the core competencies and values will really help you throughout these exercises – as it's important to know how you should be approaching them and what you should be saying.

Top tip

- It will be quite common in a situation like this for the actor(s) to use body language and perhaps also props. For example, the girl in the above scenario might be fidgeting or doodling on a piece of paper. Don't let this distract you. If the girl is engaging with your approach it may also be advisable not to ask her to stop doodling – as it might be that this is what's helping her in a potentially stressful scenario.

Video Exercises

Brand new to the assessment centre, are the video exercises. Here you are required to watch 2 scenarios. Each scenario has 3 clips in total, with a series of questions following each clip. Usually the clips are around 5 minutes in length. The way in which you watch these clips can vary. Sometimes it will be shown on your iPad, but other times the police will play the clip on a large screen.

You will not be allowed to take any notes during the videos that are played. Your task is to answer the questions as accurately as possible, based on what you remember from the video. So, your attention to detail is crucial here. You will be asked questions based on details from the scene, for example:

- What colour socks was the victim wearing?

- How many of the windows were closed?

- Which of the following items were missing?

All of the questions are multiple-choice based.

The second scenario focuses around your understanding of the police values. You will be given three clips, the same as before, showing police officers dealing with an incident. You'll then be asked questions such as:

- Do you think the police officer handled this in the correct way?

- What could the police officer have done differently in this situation?

Again, the questions will be multiple-choice based.

Since you will be answering these questions using a tablet/iPad, the tablet will proceed to auto-score all of your answers based on the competencies/values. As before, you will be given a mark from 1-5, with 5 being the highest. You won't be able to see the score, obviously.

While we can't provide you with video exercises in this guide, we have created a series of text-based exercises, which should give you a great chance to practice observation and attention to detail. Our exercises combine elements from BOTH of the above tests.

Have a go at the following exercises and then compare your answers with ours.

Interactive Video Exercises (Video-based Test)

Extract 1: Part 1

Read through the following extract, and then turn over and answer the questions that follow. You have 60 seconds to read the passage. DO NOT turn back to the passage once the 30 seconds have passed.

You have been called to a house in Croydon. A man, who owns the house, called the police, after allegedly receiving threats from his neighbours. The man is named Mr Falcon. He claims that he does not get on with his neighbours, and that after several disagreements, one of his neighbours broke into his house and threatened him. This is not the first time the police have had to deal with an incident such as this involving Mr Falcon, and many of his neighbours have complained about his behaviour – accusing him of being uncooperative and deliberately provocative.

When you walk into the property, the first thing you notice is that there is smashed glass all over the floor. Next to the right-hand window is a ball-peen hammer. The hammer is wrapped in plastic packaging, and has a label attached to it. There is a TV in the corner of the room, which is switched on, and playing the channel 2 news. There is a green leather armchair on the other side of the room, and on the armrest there is a noticeable sticky brown mark. On the floor are several empty crisp packets, and on the window sill is an empty jam jar.

Mr Falcon is demanding that the police arrest his neighbour, put him in a cell and throw away the key.

Now, turn over the page. Do not come back to this passage until you have answered ALL of the following three questions:

Q1. Next to the right-hand window, was what tool?

A – A decorating ruler

B – A spanner

C – A painting roller

D – A hammer

Q2. What colour and material was the armchair?

A – Green wool

B – Red leather

C – Green leather

D – Red wool

Q3. What object could be seen on the window sill?

A – A potted plant

B – A folded, orange jumper

C – A bowl of fruit

D – A jam jar

Extract 1: Part 2

Read through the below extract, and then turn over and answer the questions that follow. You have 60 seconds to read the passage. DO NOT turn back to the passage once the 60 seconds have passed.

Next, you go and see the neighbour – Mr Jennings. He seems warm and friendly when he opens the door, and shakes your hand firmly. As you walk into the kitchen, there is a long wooden table. On the wooden table, you notice that there is a receipt. Closer inspection reveals that this is a receipt for a hammer.

Mr Jennings offers you a hot beverage. You decline. There is a green mug on the kitchen counter. On the fridge is a drawing of a tree, with the words 'OUR GARDEN' written above it. There is a young child playing with a stuffed animal in the kitchen. The child is aged five, and is named Melanie. When you question the man about the incident next door, he seems shocked. He tells you that he has no idea what his neighbour is talking about, and informs you that he has been indoors all afternoon. Melanie asks why her daddy is lying. Upon this, Mr Jennings becomes very angry and tells her to shut up.

When you question Mr Jennings about his relationship with his neighbour, he informs you that Mr Falcon is an absolute nuisance, and that all the neighbours hate him. He claims that if somebody had broken into Mr Falcon's home, then he probably deserved it.

Now, turn over the page. Do not come back to this passage until you have answered ALL of the following three questions:

Q4. On the man's fridge was a drawing. What did the words on the drawing say?

A – Our home

B – The garden

C – The lawn

D – Our garden

Q5. Which of the following conclusions can be drawn from the above passage?

A – Melanie thinks that her father is lying about staying in all afternoon.

B – Melanie thinks that her father broke into Mr Falcon's home.

C – Melanie is unhappy with the quality of her stuffed toys.

D – Melanie does not like Mr Falcon.

Q6. Which of the following can be seen on the kitchen table?

A – A stuffed animal.

B – Plates and cutlery.

C – A jam jar

D – A receipt.

Extract 1: Part 3

Read through the below extract, and then turn over and answer the questions that follow. You have 30 seconds to read the passage. DO NOT turn back to the passage once the 30 seconds have passed.

As you leave Mr Jennings's house, one of the other neighbours approaches you. Her name is Mrs Bradshaw, and she has strawberry blonde hair. She informs you that she saw Mr Jennings smashing the window of Mr Falcon's home, with a hammer. However, she claims that Mr Falcon thoroughly deserved to have his window smashed, and that his behaviour for the past few weeks has been deliberately provocative. As she speaks to you, she scoops down and picks up a ginger tabby cat, whom she introduces as 'Tibbles'. The neighbour tells you that Mr Falcon hates cats, and leaves traps to try and snare them should they enter his garden. She labels him 'a cruel and nasty man', and tells you that the rest of the neighbourhood shares her opinion.

Your partner takes Mrs Bradshaw to one side and accuses her of helping Mr Jennings to smash the window. When Mrs Bradshaw angrily refutes this accusation, your partner tells her that he would like to take her to the station to answer some questions.

Following this incident, Mr Falcon pressed charges against Mr Jennings, for criminal damage.

Now, turn over the page. Do not come back to this passage until you have answered ALL of the following five questions:

Q7. What was the name of the female neighbour?

A – Mrs Bradley

B – Mrs Bradford

C – Mrs Bradshaw

D – Mrs Bradlaw

Q8. Which of the following words did the neighbour use to describe Mr Falcon?

A – 'Cruel' and 'evil'

B – 'Sadistic' and 'manipulative'

C – 'Nasty' and 'provocative'

D – 'Cruel' and 'sick'

Q9. Which of the following statements is definitively true?

A – 'Nobody saw Mr Jennings smashing Mr Falcon's window.'

B – 'The female neighbour owned a cat, called Tibbles.'

C – 'The female neighbour had brown hair.'

D – 'The female neighbour believes that Mr Falcon deserved to have his window smashed.'

Q10. Which of the following do you agree with, in relation to your partner's behaviour?

A – Your partner was correct to accuse Mrs Bradshaw of helping to smash the window.

B – Your partner had no grounds to question Mrs Bradshaw about the incident.

C – Your partner should have placed Mrs Bradshaw under arrest for acting angrily towards a police officer.

D – Your partner's behaviour towards Mrs Bradshaw was unacceptable.

Q11. Which of the following approaches do you believe your partner could have taken?

A – He could have pinned Mrs Bradshaw to the floor and administered an arrest.

B – He could have informed Mrs Bradshaw that her behaviour amounted to slander and that she could be held liable for such comments.

C – He could have thanked Mrs Bradshaw for providing the police with additional information.

D – He could have asked Mrs Bradshaw whether she'd mind coming along to the station, for extra questioning.

Extract 2: Part 1

Read through the following extract, and then turn over and answer the questions that follow. You have 60 seconds to read the passage. DO NOT turn back to the passage once the 60 seconds have passed.

You have been asked to attend the scene of a printing office, in London. It appears that one of the staff members is behaving extremely irrationally, and the other members of the team are extremely concerned about her behaviour. They are so concerned that they've called the police to deal with the matter.

When you arrive at the office, you can immediately see that the staff member in question has caused an enormous mess. There is a glass trophy cabinet laying on its side, which has smashed, and various awards are all over the floor. The other members of the team inform you that the woman is in an office to the right – you can hear her yelling:

'It's outrageous. I should have won that award...ME! Who the hell is Kathy Barnes? Some nobody, that's who!'

The woman's teammates explain that their colleague was expecting to win a national printing award today, but only came in second place. As a result, she became extremely angry. The woman's desk is on the far-right hand side of the office. On her desk there is a pink fluffy toy, a yellow mug and a blank writing pad.

Now, turn over the page. Do not come back to this passage until you have answered ALL of the following three questions:

Q1. Why was the woman angry?

A – She wanted a pay rise, and didn't get one.

B – She was having a bad hair day.

C – Her husband had just divorced her.

D – She came in second place for an award.

Q2. The cabinet on the floor was used to hold which items?

A – Liquor

B – Books

C – Photographs

D – Various awards

Q3. What colour was the toy on the woman's desk?

A – Green

B – Pink

C – Red

D – Blue

Extract 2: Part 2

Read through the below extract, and then turn over and answer the questions that follow. You have 60 seconds to read the passage. DO NOT turn back to the passage once the 60 seconds have passed.

The woman comes out of the office. She is still very angry, and does not appear to be calming down. Despite her colleague's attempts to relax her, she starts shouting at everyone in the office, demanding that they leave. The woman is wearing a red jumper, with a stag brooch.

One of the woman's colleagues, Wendy, informs her that she is being a sore loser. In response, the woman tells her to shut up or she'll get a smack.

You approach the woman, telling her to calm down. She takes one look at you and starts sobbing wildly. She begs the police not to arrest her, but to go and arrest 'that cow Kathy Barnes who stole my award.'

Your partner takes the woman into a back room to try and calm her down. Meanwhile, you help the rest of the staff with picking up the award cabinet.

Now, turn over the page. Do not come back to this passage until you have answered ALL of the following three questions:

Q4. What colour was the woman's jumper?

A – Purple

B – Green

C – Blue

D – Red

Q5. Who does the woman blame for upsetting her?

A – Michelle Smith

B – Steve Johnson

C – Kathy Barnes

D – Jordon Cooke

Q6. Which of the following is the woman causing trouble accused of?

A – Assaulting her colleague

B – Being a sore loser

C – Drink driving

D – Discrimination

Extract 2: Part 3

Read through the below extract, and then turn over and answer the questions that follow. You have 60 seconds to read the passage. DO NOT turn back to the passage once the 60 seconds have passed.

Whilst you are helping to clear up the glass cabinet, your colleague emerges from the back room with the distressed woman. She appears to have calmed down now.

She addresses the room:

'Guys, I just want to say I'm really sorry. And Wendy...'

Suddenly, the woman launches across the room. She grabs Wendy by the back of her neck and slams her head down on the table.

'Who's a sore loser now?!' she yells.

You and your colleague immediately react. You restrain the woman whilst your colleague checks on Wendy, who appears to be unconscious and bleeding. Your colleague calls for an ambulance immediately, whilst you put the woman in handcuffs, and escort her from the premises.

Following this incident, your colleague speaks with the woman who has been arrested, informing her that she is likely to be charged with attempted murder, and could face a lengthy jail sentence of 30 years or more. He tells her that she deserves it.

The woman is later charged with assault and battery.

Now, turn over the page. Do not come back to this passage until you have answered ALL of the following five questions:

Q7. What is the name of the woman who was attacked?

A – Kathy

B – Wendy

C – Mindy

D – Emily

Q8. Which of the following charges was levelled against the perpetrator, in this incident?

A – Theft

B – Assault and Battery

C – Manslaughter

D – Dangerous Driving

Q9. Which of the following is the most likely reason for why the woman attacked her colleague?

A – She was jealous of her colleague's success.

B – Her colleague called her a bad loser.

C – She was tired and stressed after a long and difficult day.

D – She wanted to lose her job.

Q10. Which of the following do you believe to be correct?

A – Your partner was wrong to speculate on the length of the sentence that the woman would receive.

B – Your partner should have administered CPR himself, instead of calling for an ambulance.

C – Your partner should have restrained the woman, whilst you checked on Wendy.

D – The woman who was arrested should have been charged with attempted murder.

Q11. Which of the following is true?

A – Your partner's behaviour towards the woman shows that the police are a paragon of virtue and decency in society.

B – Your partner's behaviour towards the woman could bring the reputation of the police into disrepute.

C – Your partner's behaviour towards the woman demonstrates exactly why it is important for police officers to treat every person equally, regardless of how poorly they have behaved.

D – Your partner's behaviour towards the woman will impact upon the type of sentence that she receives.

Extract 3: Part 1

Read through the following extract, and then turn over and answer the questions that follow. You have 60 seconds to read the passage. DO NOT turn back to the passage once the 60 seconds have passed.

You have been called to a flat in Manchester. The woman who called the police, who is a resident of the flat, has arrived home to find her boyfriend dead. She is extremely distressed.

When you enter the flat, you quickly notice that there is a strong smell of alcohol. This appears to have been caused by several open bottles of wine, which are laying on the kitchen worktop. At least half of them have been drunk from. Additionally, there are a number of burnt out cigarettes on the carpet.

The body of the victim is in the bathroom. He is a white male, and died whilst in the bath. There is a gunshot wound to his left temple.

On the floor of the bathroom is a soaking wet green towel, and an open bottle of shampoo. The shampoo has leaked all over the floor. Next to the bottle of shampoo is a bottle of hair conditioner, which has clearly not been opened.

The woman claims that she only left the house for 10 minutes, to go to the shops, and that her boyfriend was alive and well when she left.

Now, turn over the page. Do not come back to this passage until you have answered ALL of the following three questions:

Q1. Based on the passage, which of the following is definitively NOT true?

A – On the bathroom floor there was a blue towel and an open bottle of shampoo.

B – There were a number of burnt out cigarettes on the carpet.

C – The woman left the house for 10 minutes, and then came back to find her boyfriend dead.

D – The man was found dead in the bath.

Q2. Which of the following was found within the house?

A – Open bottles of wine and a bottle of hair conditioner.

B – A black hairdryer.

C – A half-eaten birthday cake and a tin of beans.,

D – Four tabby cats.

Q3. Where is the flat?

A – Wigan

B – Doncaster

C – Maidstone

D – Manchester

Extract 3: Part 2

Your partner immediately calls an ambulance. The woman is extremely upset, and appears to be quite hysterical. You sit down with her to have a chat. The woman tells you that she was due to be getting married to the victim in two days' time. She tells you that she has spent an awful lot of money on the wedding, and now she will be unable to get a refund.

The woman has left her shopping receipt on the table. You examine this. At the shops today, the woman bought 3 pints of milk, a box of cereal and some wash proof plasters. She also bought bin liners and bleach. The receipt is from 3 hours ago.

When you question the woman over the time frame, she becomes very defensive. She knocks over a bottle of green hair dye in frustration.

Now, turn over the page. Do not come back to this passage until you have answered ALL of the following three questions:

Q4. Which of the following did the woman purchase from the shops?

A – Bin liners, a carton of grapefruit juice and a box of cereal.

B – Bleach, 2 pints of milk and some wash proof plasters.

C – Bin liners, bleach and a box of cereal.

D – Two cartons of apple juice, a box of cereal and some plasters.

Q5. Which of the following reasons was given for the woman being upset?

A – She would now need to pay the costs for a funeral.

B – She would now need to spend time going to court.

C – She was now under suspicion for murder.

D – She would now be unable to get a refund on her wedding payment.

Q6. What colour was the bottle of hair dye?

A – Red

B – Green

C – Blue

D – Black

Extract 3: Part 3

Your partner takes you to one side and asks you for a quiet chat. He informs you that he found a gun in the bedroom. He says that the gun was hidden in a blue pillowcase. He also says that he found a diary in the same pillowcase, in which was written threatening messages.

The woman suddenly stands up. She informs you that she'll need to leave now, and starts grabbing her stuff to go. Your partner stands in front of the door. He tells her that she will be unable to leave, and that she has some serious questions to answer.

The woman sits back down and starts sobbing.

'I didn't mean to kill him. I just wanted to scare him a bit...but then the gun accidentally went off.'

At this point, the ambulance arrives. Two paramedics enter the room, one male and one female. At this point, the woman informs you and your partner that she wants to take her own life.

Your partner places the woman under arrest. One of the paramedics then approaches him, and asks what will happen to the woman. Despite the woman still being in the room, your partner informs the paramedic that the woman will be tried and convicted for murder, and could even receive the death penalty.

Now, turn over the page. Do not come back to this passage until you have answered ALL of the following five questions:

Q7. What was the gender of the paramedics?

A – Two males, two females.

B – Three females.

C – Four males

D – One male, one female.

Q8. Where did your partner find the woman's diary?

A – Under her bed.

B – In her sock drawer.

C – In a pillowcase.

D – On the table.

Q9. What was the woman's explanation for her behaviour?

A – She was being abused by her husband, and shot him.

B – She wanted to frame someone else for murder.

C – She was trying to scare her husband, and accidentally shot him.

D – She thought that it was a toy gun.

Q10. Which of the following do you believe is true?

A – Your partner should have taken the woman's previous comment into consideration, when speaking about the death penalty.

B – Your partner is insensitive to say that the woman will receive the death penalty, as the case has not even gone to court yet.

C – You and your partner should have contacted a mental health specialist, instead of arresting the woman.

D – Your partner was wrong to speculate that the woman committed murder.

Q11. Which of the following is the most accurate summary of why your partner should not have discussed the details of the case with the paramedic:

A – Your partner has every right to discuss the details of the case with the paramedic, since the paramedic will likely need to provide evidence in court.

B – Your partner should not have discussed the details of the case with the paramedic, since all you have at the moment is circumstantial evidence.

C – The paramedic has nothing to do with the actual arrest, and is there to provide medical assistance/forensic analysis on the murder victim.

D – The paramedic has not provided either you or your partner with reliable evidence that they are a qualified medical professional.

Answers

Extract 1, Part 1:	Extract 1, Part 2:	Extract 1, Part 3:
1. D	4. A	7. C
2. C	5. A	8. C
3. D	6. B	9. D
		10. D
		11. C

Extract 2, Part 1:	Extract 2, Part 2:	Extract 2, Part 3:
1. D	4. D	7. B
2. D	5. C	8. B
3. B	6. B	9. B
		10. A
		11. B

Extract 3, Part 1:	Extract 3, Part 2:	Extract 3, Part 3:
1. A	4. C	7. D
2. A	5. D	8. C
3. D	6. B	9. C
		10. A
		11. C

Virtual Reality Exercise

The next test that you will need to take is brand new to the assessment centre, and is called the Virtual Reality Exercise. This exercise lasts for approximately 10 minutes.

The Virtual Reality Exercise essentially requires you to work in a coordinated fashion with another candidate, to resolve a problem. One person will wear a virtual reality headset, which will place them in a particular environment – such as a set of rooms. The other person will use their iPad, which contains a map/picture of how the room should look.

One person will play the role of control and the other person will play the role of ground. Together you will need to decide which of you will play which role. You won't be marked on this conversation, but you will need to have the conversation in front of the assessors. The two roles are as follows:

- Control's job is to provide key information and navigational help to Ground. You will essentially need to guide Ground around the room/virtual reality environment, helping them to reach the finishing marker.

- Ground's role is to verbally relay what they can see using the virtual reality headset, to Control.

Here's how the assessment will be structured:

First of all, you'll be briefed on the operation. For example, you'll be told that you are visiting the scene of a suspected burglary.

Both participants will sit down. Ground will be given a virtual reality headset, and can then move and turn to see a more detailed view of the room that the headset depicts. Ground will be given very limited info about exactly where they are and what should be in the rooms. Control will be given an iPad which shows a detailed map or picture of how the room should look.

There will be deliberate differences between how the room is meant to look on the iPad, and what Ground sees using the virtual reality headset. The two candidates will be expected to communicate and remember these differences. Furthermore, Control will be given a list of items on their iPad, detailing items that should be present within the room, and also information about the location where Ground is. Control will be expected to communicate these to Ground.

What does this assessment test?

The Virtual Reality Exercise is a direct test of your teamwork skills, and your communication abilities. Both candidates need to work together to pass the test, and will need to be constantly communicating clearly and effectively with each other.

Below is a short example of what we mean by this:

Ground: Okay, I am in what looks like a lounge area. There is a red sofa, and a child's stuffed animal on the carpet.

Control: That's great, you are indeed in the lounge. Can you please confirm for me that there is also a picture of a pink elephant on the wall?

Ground: Yes, that's right, I see it! The picture is above the sofa.

Control: Great. Next to the sofa there should also be a wooden table. Do you see that?

Ground: There is no wooden table…but there is a bottle of wine on the floor next to the sofa.

Control: Ah, the intelligence I have here says that there should be a wooden table. Can you confirm that's not the case?

Ground: I can confirm, there's no wooden table.

Following the exercise, the assessors will ask you a series of questions, usually 3 or 4, focusing on areas such as:

- What were the locations you attended?

- What discrepancies did you notice between the intelligence provided, and what was at the scene?

- Did you notice anything out of place or strange?

Although it's important to get these right, remember that the biggest focus of this exercise is on your teamwork and coordination.

Below we have provided you with two sample exercises. While we can't give you an actual virtual reality test, we have created an assessment which challenges the same skills as the real thing, and requires constant communication between the two parties. See if you can get a friend to do these with you.

Take a look at the following example:

Key

 Start (arrow indicates initial starting direction. Only ground sees the starting location)

 Finish (only control gets to see the finishing location)

 Obstruction (text inside indicates nature of obstruction). **IMPORTANT: you cannot pass through obstructed roads.**

Sitepoint (you should aim to visit all sitepoints and confirm these with each other)

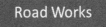

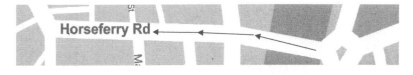

One way system (one way begins at the first arrow, not at the start of that road. For example you are allowed to cross straight over a one way road without entering the one way system)

EXAMPLE

Remember you should only see one map. Control should only see the map labelled Control, and the same for Ground.

The example communication for this is on the next page. Take a look at the below maps, and how the example communication corresponds to them, to familiarise yourself before taking the test.

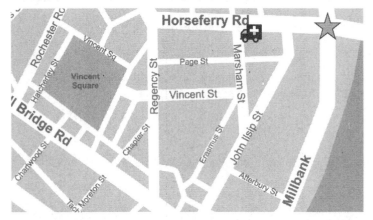

CONTROL

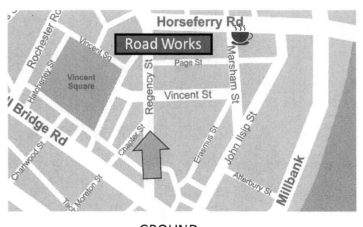

GROUND

EXAMPLE COMMUNICATION:

In the example, the communication may run like this:

C: Ground, please can you confirm which street you are on.

G: I can confirm I am on Regency Street facing North.

C: Great. Please continue North to the end of Regency Street and then head East onto Horseferry Road.

G: Negative, there are road works preventing access to Horseferry Road. I can turn around and make access through Page Street? Please confirm.

C: Affirmative Ground, please make your way through Page Street. At the end of the road are you able to make a left to head north on Marsham Street?

G: I can confirm I am heading East on Page Street. I am able to head north on Marsham Street and have reached a junction.

C: Before you continue, please can you confirm you see a ambulance on the junction between Marsham street and Horseferry Road?

G: Negative, there is no ambulance, but there is a coffee shop at that location.

C: Received, thank you. Please can you take a right onto Horseferry Road heading East. Please head to the first crossroads and you will have reached your destination.

G: Control, I can confirm I have reached my destination.

In the following exercise you will be given a map. One person should play the role of Control and the other person should play the role of 'Ground'. The main aim of the exercise is to get Ground to the finishing destination via communication with Control.

Both Control and Ground get a map of the same location, but different information will be available on each map (e.g. Ground can see heavy traffic which Control may not be aware of). Control gets to see the finishing destination and Ground gets to see the starting location.

This task is designed to test your team working, logical thinking, and communication skills. You should work on a road-by-road basis and NOT skip ahead. Be aware, certain elements might be missing on each map. It is up to you to work together to fill in the blanks and make it to your destination in the most efficient way.

Additionally, Control has a checklist of places that Ground needs to visit and verify are there (again road-by-road – do not skip ahead, you can only call/name a location once you're on the same street). If they aren't there, this should be mentally noted but not written down. You will be asked questions about your journey at the end of the exercise.

Make sure to set a timer. You should aim to complete the exercise within 7 minutes.

HOW TO COMPLETE THIS EXERCISE
1.   Open the book to show both maps, face each other with the book in the middle.
2.   Cut out the pages along the dotted line (each map will be labeled 'Ground' or 'Control').
3.   Download the maps at the following link: **www.PoliceVRTest.co.uk** Once you are on this page don't forget to enter the following code: **POLICEVR28**

CONTROL

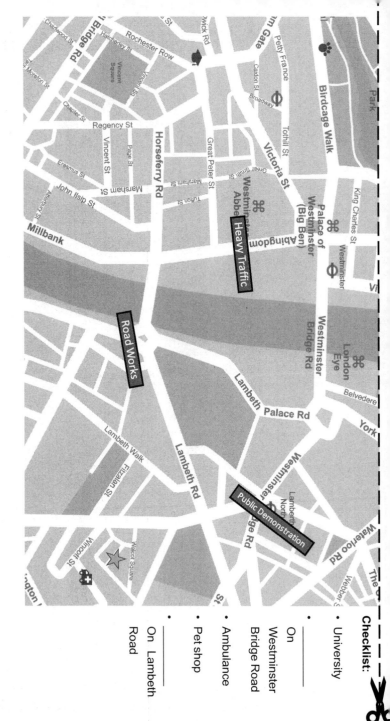

Checklist:

- University
- _____
- On Westminster Bridge Road
- Ambulance
- Pet shop
- _____
- On Lambeth Road

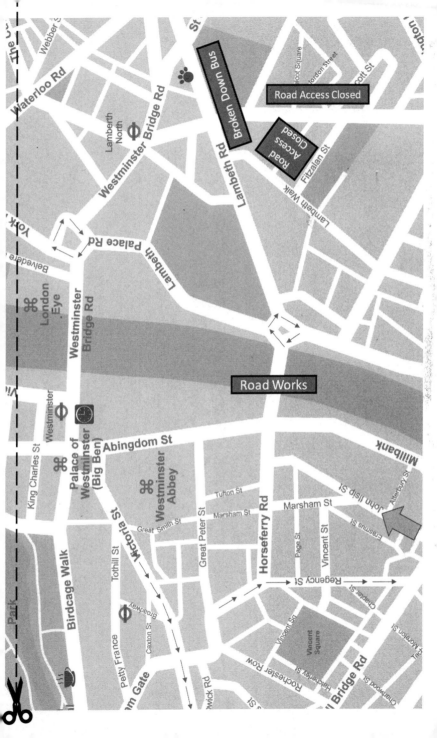

Broken Down Bus

Road Access Closed

Road Access Closed

Road Works

GROUND

QUESTIONS

Now try your best to answer the following questions together from memory. You are not allowed to look at the map, your checklist or any notes you may have made.

- Which road was Ground's destination point?

- Which two sitepoints had swapped location on Ground's Map compared to Control's map?

- What locations/sitepoints were missing from Control's map?

- What locations/sitepoints were missing from Ground's map?

Answer

Obviously, there are different routes that you could have taken, but here is one suggested route:

Ground: I am facing north east on John Ilsip Street.

Control: Okay, great. Please head north and turn onto Marsham Street.

Ground: I am now on Horseferry Road.

Control: Okay, please head west on Horseferry Road and take the second turning on your right, travelling North onto Marsham Street.

Ground: Okay, I am on Marsham Street

Control: Now that you've reached Marsham Street, go north onto Great Peter Street and then travel East, until you reach the university on the corner.

Ground: There is no university.

Control: Oh, my intel says that there should be a university at the end of Great Peter Street, at the top of Rochester Row.

Ground: I can confirm there's no university here.

Control: Alright, thanks. Go north past Victoria Street until you reach Petty France, turn east onto Petty France and then keep going East onto Tothill Street. Following that, take the north exit onto Birdcage Walk.

Ground: I have arrived on Birdcage Walk.

Control: Okay, go East until you reach the pet shop, please.

Ground: There is no pet shop here.

Control: No pet shop? It says on my intel that there should be on at the end of road.

Ground: No pet shop, but there is a coffee shop.

Control: Okay, thank you for that. Go back east on Birdcage Walk, and keep going past the palace of Westminster, until you reach Westminster Bridge Road.

Ground: I have now reached Westminster Bridge Road. At the start of this road there was a clocktower.

Control: Ah, okay. I don't have on my map. Thanks for letting me know. Okay, you should now see a roundabout. Take the south turnoff from the roundabout onto Lambeth Palace Road.

Ground: Done. I am now on Lambeth Palace Road!

Control: Okay, great. Take the first exit on this road, then head east, and then south until you get onto Lambeth Road.

Ground: Okay…I am now on Lambeth Road.

Control: At the crossroads, take the first exit southbound, travelling down to Walcot Square.

Ground: I can't do that, as there is a broken-down bus in the way, opposite the pet shop.

Control: There is a pet shop?

Ground: Yes, at the end of Lambeth Road.

Control: Ah, okay, I don't have that on my map. Can you go back onto Lambeth Road, and then head south down to Lambeth Walk?

Ground: I can. Heading onto Lambeth Walk now.

Control: Right, take the second exit on Lambeth Walk, onto Fitzalan Street, once you reach the end of Fitzalan Street travel south then take the first exit onto Wincott Street. Take the north east turning from Wincott Street, and you should see an ambulance.

Ground: There's no ambulance here.

Control: Oh really? Okay, well I have an ambulance on mine. In any case, head back the way you came onto Wincott Street, then go north until until you reach the turn off for Walcot Square.

Ground: I can't turn onto Walcot Square, as it says road access closed.

Control: Alright. Keep travelling north and take the next road on your right after Walcot Square.

Ground: Okay.

Control: Travel south west and turn onto the second road on your right.

Ground: I am on Jordon Street.

Answers to Questions

Q1. Which road was Ground's destination point?

Jordon Street

Q2. Which two sitepoints had swapped location on Ground's Map compared to Control's map?

The coffee shop and the pet shop.

Q3. What locations/sitepoints were missing from Control's map?

The clocktower and the coffee shop

Q4. What locations/sitepoints were missing from Ground's map?

The university and the ambulance.

SAMPLE ROUTE:

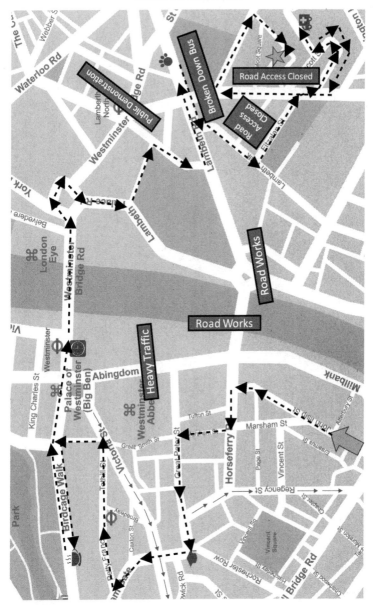

Now take the same approach for the next exercise!

CONTROL

Checklist:

- University
- Coffee shop
- Ambulance

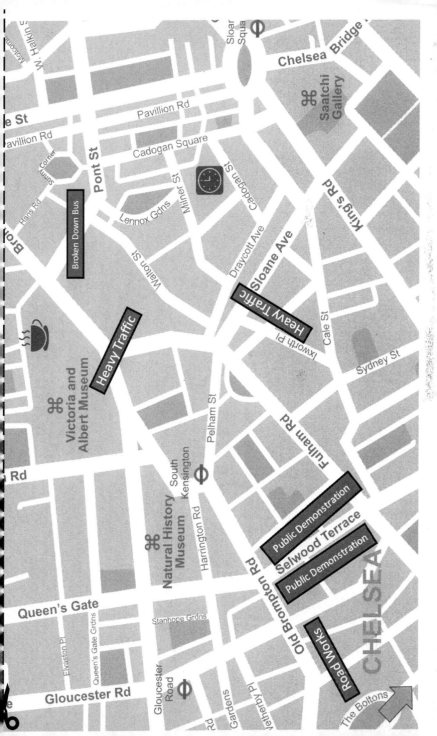

GROUND

QUESTIONS

Now try your best to answer the following questions together from memory. You are not allowed to look at the map, your checklist or any notes you may have made.

- Which road was Ground's destination point?

- Which sitepoint was missing from Control's map?

- What sitepoint did Control have, that Ground didn't have?

Answer

Ground: I am on The Boltons, facing south east.

Control: Okay, great. Head east into Chelsea, turn right at the end of the road then travel north east. Take the second turn on your left onto Selwood Terrace.

Ground: I am on Selwood Terrace.

Control: Okay. Head north towards Old Brompton Road, and then keep going north, crossing straight over the crossroad at Harrington Road. Turn right at the next crossroad and travel until you reach the Natural History Museum.

Ground: I'm at the Natural History Museum.

Control: Opposite you, you should see an ambulance.

Ground: Nope, there's no ambulance here.

Control: Ah, okay. There's an ambulance opposite the museum on my map. Head back past the museum to the crossroad and travel north onto Queens Gate. Then take the second exit on the right, and go straight on until you reach the Victoria and Albert Museum.

Ground: I have reached the Victoria and Albert Museum.

Control: Okay, head south past the Museum, and head south west at the end of the road, keep going to South Kensington underground station.

Ground: I'm at South Kensington underground station. Where do I go now?

Control: Head south until you reach Pelham Street, then go east.

Ground: Okay

Control: Head north and take an immediate onto Draycott Avenue.

Ground: Right, I'm at Draycott Avenue.

Control: Travel east along Draycott Ave then turn north east onto

Cadogan Street, where you should see a clock tower.

Ground: There's a university, but not a clock tower.

Control: That's interesting, my intel says otherwise. Okay, go to the end of the street and then head north up Cadogan Square, until you get to Pont Street.

Ground: Alright.

Control: Follow Pont Street north west

Ground: I can't do that, there's a broken-down bus.

Control: Oh dear, that doesn't appear on mine. Okay, do you see a roundabout straight ahead?

Ground: Yes.

Control: Go round the roundabout, take the north east exit onto Hans Road. At the end of Hans Road head south west, then take the second north west exit. Go up the road. You should see a coffee shop.

Ground: I do see a coffee shop!

Control: Okay, great. Now head back the way you came, back down Hans Road, going onto the roundabout. Take the north exit at the top of the roundabout, and you are at your destination.

Ground: Okay, I am at Sunny Corner.

Answers to Questions

Q1. Which road was Ground's destination point?

Sunny Corner

Q2. Which sitepoint was missing from Control's map?

The clocktower

Q3. What sitepoint did Control have, that Ground didn't have?

The ambulance

SAMPLE ROUTE:

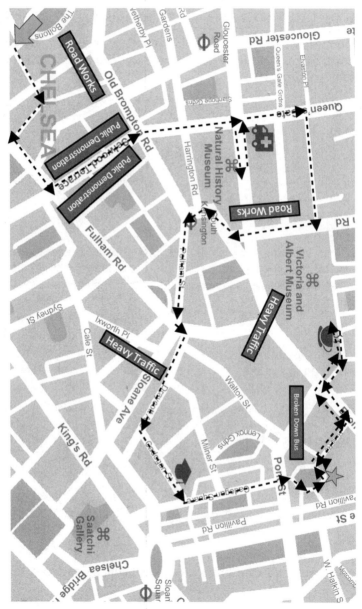

Written Exercise

Finally, we have the written exercise. This exercise is essentially a variation on an old police assessment centre test, where you would be writing a response in the role of the customer services officer of a shopping centre. You will have 30 minutes to complete the written exercise.

The exercise is quite different now. For a start, you will be conducting the entire exercise on your iPad. This means that you need to be absolutely on-point with all your grammar, spelling and punctuation, as there's no spellchecking on an iPad.

To start the exercise, you'll be asked to call on a button labelled 'Stop and Search'. Once you click this, the exercise will begin.

Immediately appearing on your screen will be a message from your police sergeant, informing you of a general policing matter. For example, the message might be telling you that they've increased foot patrols in a certain vicinity – to stamp out crimes – or that the police are increasing the number of people whom they are stopping and searching – again in a bid to stamp out crime. There will generally be a caveat following this. For example, the sergeant will tell you that someone has taken umbrage with the police's new approach, and has written to him to complain. This person might be a shopping centre owner, a member of the local council, etc.

Along with the message from your sergeant, you'll be given a number of a cards and a highlighter. The cards will contain extra information about the task. For example, they might contain the letter of complaint that has been sent to the sergeant, they might complain further feedback from various people, and they might contain data and crime statistics related to the matter.

Your task is to respond to the letter of complaint that the Sergeant has received, addressing all of the issues raised, either persuading the person of the benefits of the approach or offering alternative solutions.

The central aim of this exercise is to test the following aspects:

- The quality of your written communication.

- Your trainability, and ability to understand stop and search law.

- Your ability to problem solve.

- Your customer handling skills.

Your written response will be scored against the core values and competencies. You will be given a score of 1-5, with 5 being the highest, in each competency/value.

Now, let's look at some example exercises. We've gone through the first one for you, just to give you an idea of how to approach these.

Example Exercise 1

Read all of the information provided, and then respond to the complaint letter.

Message from Sergeant

New Message   – ✗ ✕

From Walker@Ficshirepolice.com   Cc Bcc

Subject   Responding to Mrs Smith

Dear PC Briggs,

As you know, as of May 1st we have beefed up foot patrols on North Ficshire High Street. This is codenamed Operation Beefeater. There's been a sharp increase in physical violence involving youths recently, and the police are under huge pressure to stop this from happening. After a series of stabbings, I've also authorised officers to conduct stop and search on anyone whom they feel looks intimidating or threatening. I truly think this is the best way to increase confidence in the police with the community of North Ficshire.

Unfortunately, some people aren't in agreement with this new approach. Specifically, I've received a written complaint from Shirley Smith of Odds'N'Ends tailoring – which is a popular store on the High Street. She claims that the presence of extra officers is scaring away her customers, and that it's really intimidating. Furthermore, she says that her son was stopped unfairly by officers, and that he is traumatised by the incident. I've attached her letter for you to look at, and also a case file for her son – who has a pretty terrible track record. Along with this, we've also received a couple of other complaints from shop owners, but I can deal with these. I've attached some of their feedback though, just to give you an idea of what they are saying.

Please could you respond to Mrs Smith, explaining exactly why the stop and searches, plus the extra officers, are warranted. I've also attached a sheet which thoroughly debunks her claims about her son.

Sincerely,

Sergeant Walker

Reply   ■ | ▾

Attachment 1

10 Ficshire Avenue
Ficshire
FO1 FC8

Ficshire Police Department
1 Ficshire Way,
Ficshire,
FOO OFC

10th May

COMPLAINT

To whom it may concern,

I am writing to express my sincere regret at the way the police in North Ficshire have conducted themselves over the past 4 weeks. First of all, as I'm aware, the police are increasing foot patrols in the area. We received a newsletter about this, but I had absolutely no chance to give feedback. How can the police operate like this? They should be transparent with the general public. It goes without saying that the increased number of police officers in the area has detracted from my customers, and business has been seriously down as a result. It's really intimidating to see officers all over the place. Especially for new visitors to the town – this makes it look as if North Ficshire is an absolute warzone.

Secondly, on a more personal note, my son was forced to undergo a 'stop and search' routine by officers in the area. This was both unprovoked and humiliating for him. The officers found no evidence to suggest that he was a threat, and to my knowledge he was not behaving in any way that would have brought about this assumption.

I find all of this absolutely unacceptable, and I demand to know what you are going to do about it.

Shirley Smith,

Owner of Odds'N'Ends.

How To Look At This

So, you've read the first attachment. As mentioned, you'll be given a highlighter pen during the assessment, so now you need to work out exactly which parts to highlight. Remember that you are going to be responding to this disputing Mrs Smith's claims, but still presenting a polite and responsible outlook. You need to sort out the relevant information from the non-relevant. With this in mind, below we've highlighted the parts that we think will be the most important moving forward:

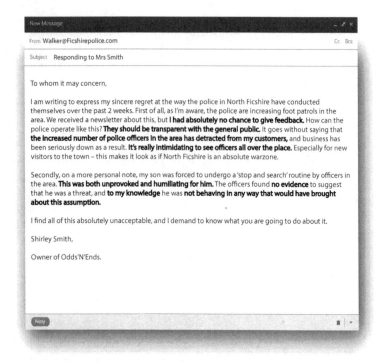

New Message

From Walker@Ficshirepolice.com   Cc Bcc

Subject   Responding to Mrs Smith

To whom it may concern,

I am writing to express my sincere regret at the way the police in North Ficshire have conducted themselves over the past 2 weeks. First of all, as I'm aware, the police are increasing foot patrols in the area. We received a newsletter about this, but **I had absolutely no chance to give feedback.** How can the police operate like this? **They should be transparent with the general public.** It goes without saying that **the increased number of police officers in the area has detracted from my customers,** and business has been seriously down as a result. **It's really intimidating to see officers all over the place.** Especially for new visitors to the town – this makes it look as if North Ficshire is an absolute warzone.

Secondly, on a more personal note, my son was forced to undergo a 'stop and search' routine by officers in the area. **This was both unprovoked and humiliating for him.** The officers found **no evidence** to suggest that he was a threat, and **to my knowledge** he was **not behaving in any way that would have brought about this assumption.**

I find all of this absolutely unacceptable, and I demand to know what you are going to do about it.

Shirley Smith,

Owner of Odds'N'Ends.

Reply

Now, let's move onto the second attachment.

Attachment 2

Below is a set of statistics and data for North Ficshire High Street, for this year. The data sheet includes monthly statistics for crime.

JANUARY

TOTAL NUMBER OF CRIMES COMMITTED: 76

Arson – 3%

Burglary – 11%

Unlawful possession of weapons – 46%

Physical violence or battery – 40%

FEBRUARY

TOTAL NUMBER OF CRIMES COMMITTED: 136

Arson – 2%

Rape – 5%

Physical violence or battery – 30%

Aggravated assault – 13%

Unlawful possession of weapons – 50%

MARCH

TOTAL NUMBER OF CRIMES COMMITTED: 206

Unlawful possession of weapons – 40%

Aggravated assault – 50%

Theft – 5%

Physical violence or battery – 5%

APRIL

TOTAL NUMBER OF CRIMES COMMITTED: 311

Physical violence or battery – 60%

Unlawful possession of weapons – 30%

Aggravated assault – 10%

From the month of May onwards, the police began Operation Beefeater.

MAY

TOTAL NUMBER OF CRIMES COMMITTED: 102

Physical violence or battery – 20%

Unlawful possession of weapons – 20%

Burglary – 5%

Rape – 5%

Arson – 2%

Theft – 30%

Abuse or racial hatred – 18%

How To Look At This

Clearly you can see from the above attachment that Operation Beefeater has had a significant impact. The total number of crimes committed has dropped hugely, and there has also been a huge decrease in the number of people charged with carrying unlawful weapons. This is all great information to include in your response to Shirley Smith at the end of the exercise.

Attachment 3

Below is a police report from the stop-and-search of Ben Smith, son of Shirley Smith.

INCIDENT REPORT

I was walking down North Ficshire High Street, at approximately 14:16pm, on Monday 12th May. Ahead of me, I noticed that there was a disturbance happening. Two boys were punching each other. They were on the floor, and one of them was bleeding heavily.

My partner and I quickly rushed over to intervene. We pulled the two boys apart. One of them, Ben Smith, started swearing at me. It was not the first time I have encountered Mr Smith. In fact, we have had a number of experiences with Mr Smith – none of them good. On this occasion I felt that it was entirely warranted to enforce a stop and search, under the protocols of Operation Beefeater. Mr Smith did not react well to this. In fact, he flat out refused to cooperate, only doing so when we threatened arrest. Although inspection of Mr Smith did not reveal any items which could be deemed contrary to the law, I feel that my behaviour in this circumstance was completely justified.

Signed:

PC Bradley

PC Bradley

How To Look At This

This is a very useful document. Here you have a certified report from a police officer who dealt with Mrs Smith's son, showing that the stop and search protocol was completely warranted, and that Ben Smith's behaviour was in contradiction with his mother's assertion that this was 'unprovoked'. You can use this in your final letter.

Attachment 4

Below are some views of other shop owners and members of the public, about Operation Beefeater.

OPINION POSTS

Linda Branning
Owner of Groceries4U

'So far, I am delighted with the efforts of the police in making North Ficshire a safer place. I have had feedback from customers telling me that they feel far more secure, and that they are happier coming to my store than before.'

Connect   Message   Comment

Miles Bingham
Frequent visitor to North Ficshire High Street

'I feel like the increased police presence makes everything seem a little bit intimidating. However, I'm much happier and feel much safer now than I did before. At the town council meeting where it was made clear what would happen before this was introduced, we discussed a number of things, and I feel like they've all been implemented.'

Connect   Message   Comment

Aaron Edwards
Owner of DressesforQueens

'Thanks to this new police initiative, my business is booming. Everything we discussed at the town council meeting on the 4th May has been put into place, really well actually. I'm also glad that the police invited all the shop owners, this felt very inclusive. Over the last few months, increased violence has seen things dip dramatically. This month though, it's on the up. People feel safer coming to store, and now I'm making more money.'

Connect   Message   Comment

Wendy Richards
Owner of Clay Pigeon Dynasty

'I own a company called Clay Pigeon Dynasty, which is just next door to Odds'N'Ends. In the past month, my sales have trebled, as our customers return to the street. This is definitely down to the increased police foot patrols. It's just a fact that people feel safer coming here now.'

Connect   Message   Comment

How To Look At This

Again, this is all great evidence for you to use in your response to Shirley. There is clear evidence here that the increased foot patrols have not deterred shoppers from coming to the street, as Shirley claims, and that the general public feel by in large safer and more secure as a result of this. Likewise, there is clear evidence that a meeting was held between members of the town – which is in contradiction to Shirley's claim that she had no opportunity for feedback.

Your Response

Now, you need to write out a response to Shirley. Make sure you read her letter carefully, to address every single point raised. Below we've written out a sample response, that shows how this could be done. Make sure you pay particular attention to spelling, grammar and punctuation – because you will be marked on this.

Dear Mrs Smith,

I am very sorry to hear that you are unhappy with the new police initiative, and the way that your son has been treated. The central aim of the police is to ensure that every single person feels safe, comfortable and secure, and therefore it is of great disappointment to me that you do not feel this has been accomplished. However, I do disagree with a number of your points. I will address each of these individually below:

First of all, you have claimed that you had no opportunity to give feedback on these changes. This is not the case. On the 4th May there was a town council meeting, to which all of the shop owners on North Ficshire High Street were invited. During this meeting all of the new changes were discussed, and attendees were given the chance to voice their opinions or concerns. I would like to assure you that the police operate with maximum transparency – our aim is to serve you and provide you with a safer place to live and work.

Secondly, I would like to dispute your claim that the increased numbers of officers in the area have detracted from the customer base. We have a number of references from other shop owners, who work in very close proximity to your own store, demonstrating that their sales figures and customer numbers have increased as a result of these changes. While I appreciate your view that having large numbers of officers in the area can make North Ficshire look a little intimidating, I believe that this is a marked improvement on the intimidation that violence and crime can bring. Furthermore, I am confident that our officers always conduct themselves in a polite and non-threatening manner, presenting a warm and friendly approach to the public.

Thirdly, your claims about your son are incorrect. I have taken the time to look through the case report from your son's stop and search, and I have full confidence that the officer who conducted the search did so with the appropriate authority and justification. Your son was behaving in an aggressive way, and therefore this search was completely warranted.

The new police initiative was brought in to bring peace and security to shop owners and members of the public on North Ficshire High Street. Although it is still early, our crime and data statistics indicate that there has been a marked decrease in the number of serious crimes committed since we introduced this, and therefore we are confident that we can achieve our aims.

If you do wish to provide any further feedback, then I am more than happy to accommodate for this, and would welcome any constructive comments based on our police department moving forward.

Yours sincerely,

PC Briggs.

Example Exercise 2

Now, it's your turn! Take a look through the below and see if you can construct your own response, based on the information in this exercise.

Message from Sergeant

New Message _ ⚡ x

From Walker@Ficshirepolice.com   Cc Bcc

Subject   Responding to Member of Public

Dear PC Johnson,

As you should be aware, we've recently made a sustained effort to crack down on knife crime in South Ficshire. Mainly, we've been deploying officers to work night shifts outside all of the South Ficshire clubs. The move has come in the wake of a recent spate of attacks. Most of them were attributed to drunk and disorderly behaviour, but the fact remains that these youths are actually bringing knives to clubs, and somehow getting them in.

With this in mind, we're conducting routine stop and searches during 'peak' nightlife hours – we've been searching suspected individuals before they go into the clubs, and afterwards too. So far, we've got a few, but the crimes keep happening.

I don't know what we're doing wrong, but today I received an angry letter from a nightclub owner, who says that we're hurting his business. I've also got a letter from someone who was recently stopped. I'll respond to the first one, but I want you to respond to the second one please.

Sincerely,

Sergeant Walker

Reply   🗑 ▼

Attachment 1

10 Ficshire Avenue
Ficshire
FO1 FC8

Ficshire Police Department
1 Ficshire Way,
Ficshire,
FOO OFC

16th March

COMPLAINT

To whom it may concern,

I feel that I have been treated unacceptably by certain officers within your force. Please allow me to recount the events that happened. On the night of Thursday 15th March, I was walking with my friends towards a club. Whilst entering the premises, we were approached by a male officer and his colleague. The male officer immediately demanded that we stop and submit to a search. I felt that he was extremely rude about this. I understand that knife crime is a problem in this area, but I did not deserve such impolite treatment. Regardless, since he was an officer of the law, I complied. The officer then proceeded to conduct the search on me, in a very rough manner. I sustained bruising on my knee from the physicality on his search, during which he (obviously) did not find any weapons.

Following the search, the officer did not even thank me for complying. He just grunted and walked away.

I consider this to be appalling, and I am very upset by the way this was done.

Sincerely,

James Pearson

Attachment 2

Below is a list of feedback and comments from various members of the public, surrounding the increased searches.

OPINION POLL FEEDBACK

Benjamin Broadsmith
Frequent club goer

'I am pleased that the police are conducting stop and search procedures on club-goers. For too long, knife crime has been a problem in this part of town, and it needs to stop. That being said, I feel like more could have been done to speak with members of the public about the new searches. Most people seem wholly unprepared to be searched. Naturally, they act as if they are being accused of something, when that's not really the case.'

👤 Connect   ✉ Message   💬 Comment

Melanie Waterman
Frequent club goer

'The new police checks are a load of rubbish. It's not even that they are searching us, I'm fine with that, but they are so aggressive! It's like they just come up to you and demand that you stop and do whatever you say. I've seen two friends get stopped, and it was the same both time – the police were really rude and didn't even thank her after the search, they just walked off.'

👤 Connect   ✉ Message   💬 Comment

Steve Jackson
Club owner

'The police stop and search routine isn't accomplishing anything. The bottom line is, people know if their mates are bringing knives to the club, but why would they tell the police about that when the officers are being so rude and aggressive? They're treating my customers like pieces of meat.'

👤 Connect   ✉ Message   💬 Comment

Katie Jacobs
Homeowner in South Ficshire

'I've got no problem with the police treating people like they do. What's more important, security or manners? Let them do what they've got to do, and get the knife scum out of our town.'

👤 Connect   ✉ Message   💬 Comment

Attachment 3

Below is a short extract from the South Ficshire poluice guidelines, written by an admin assistant, on how stop and search should be carried out:

FICSHIRE POLICE GUIDELINES

'…in the event that an officer believes a member of the public is carrying an unlawful item, they must take immediate action. It's important to show the person suspected that you are serious about stopping their potential behaviour, and therefore a firm approach is recommended. When searching the individual, ensure that every element of their person is inspected, including areas such as shoes and socks, for unlawful items. There is no requirement to thank the individual for allowing you to do this, as it's part of the law.'

Your Response

Now, write your response to James Pearson in the textbox below. Following that, we've included some tips on things you should have spotted.

How did you get on? Hopefully, you should have spotted that this exercise was very different to the last one. In the first exercise, we were essentially disputing the claims that a member of the public had made. In this exercise, the flaw is clearly with the police – so you should have addressed this in your answer. This will include doing things such as:

- Apologising to James, for the treatment that he received.

- Explaining to James the aims of the new initiative, using the police values and competencies to structure this.

- Assuring James that this issue will be dealt with as a matter of priority, and that you will be speaking to the Sergeant about this.

- Telling James that the reason for this mistake is down to a miscommunication in training, and assuring him that the police will be taking steps to address such behaviour in the future.

- Offering James the chance to give further feedback in future, and asking him to follow up with you about the change in police behaviour in a week or so.

Remember, the police are there to serve the public. That means making improvements to police practice based on customer feedback. You should also hopefully have noticed that the definition of how stop and search should be conducted, in attachment 3, is quite flawed and wrong. This would be one of the main areas of concern that you must bring to the Sergeant's attention.

Now that we've finished looking at the exercises, let's move onto the Assessment Centre Interview.

Assessment Centre Interview

The final stage of the assessment centre is the police interview. Just like the other exercises, the interview has undergone a significant revamp for 2018. The format is still largely the same: you'll face 4 competency-based questions, lasting 5 minutes each. However, the interview will be much more relaxed now. You'll be welcomed into the room with a handshake, and you will also get to look at the questions on your iPad. Just as before, the questions will focus largely on your past experiences and how you've demonstrated the core competencies.

Following each question, you'll receive follow up questions. For example, 'How do you think you benefitted that situation?' and 'What did you take away from your experience?'

The police interview will focus heavily on the core competencies. Each question will be focused around a specific competency, but in your response you should also endeavour to demonstrate as many of the other competencies as possible. Most of the time, this will occur naturally. For example, working collaboratively might require you to demonstrate a level of emotional awareness.

All of the questions will be situational based. This means that you will need to give a detailed account of when you have demonstrated the behaviour being asked for. Your response to each situational question must be 'specific' in nature. This means that you must provide an example where you have already been in this type of situation. During your response you should provide details of how you handled or dealt with the situation, preferably with a successful outcome.

Do not fall into the trap of providing a 'generic' response that details what you 'would do' if the situation arose, unless of course you have not been in this type of situation before. When responding to situational questions try to structure your responses in a logical and concise manner. The way to achieve this is to use the 'STAR' method of interview question response construction:

Situation. Start off your response to the interview question by explaining what the 'situation' was and who was involved.

Task. Once you have detailed the situation, explain what the 'task' was, or what needed to be done.

Action Now explain what 'action' you took, and what action others took. Also explain why you took this particular course of action.

Result. Explain to the panel what you would do differently if the same situation arose again. It is good to be reflective at the end of your responses. This demonstrates a level of maturity and it will also show the panel that you are willing to learn from every experience.

Finally, explain what the outcome or result was following your actions and those of others. Try to demonstrate in your response that the result was positive because of the action you took.

Now, let's look at some sample questions. Please note that these are NOT the exact questions that you will see during the real police interview, and you should base your own answers on your own experiences.

Sample Question 1

Q. Tell me about a time when you have demonstrated your ability to be innovative.

How To Answer

In this question, the interviewer is clearly testing the core competency of being innovative and open minded. So, you need to think about what these competency entails, before you can respond. Remember that being innovative and open minded requires a very specific mindset. You must be someone who is creative, can problem solve, and is open to new methods of police work. So, try and demonstrate all of this in your response!

Write your answer to this question in the box below, and then compare it to our sample response:

Sample Response

'Whilst working for my previous company, a business consultancy firm, I was one of the team leaders. Our team was specifically tasked with producing presentations for visiting cliental and customers, with the aim of endorsing our products and encouraging them to utilise our services.

On one occasion, my team was asked to make a presentation to a partnership agency who were considering investing a large amount of money in our company. This was a huge responsibility. Although I felt very nervous, I was confident in my ability to manage the team and produce a truly excellent presentation. I believed that, since I had given many similar presentations before, this one would be similar. I quickly got to work, assigning people individual roles and parts to present, based on their strengths. However, halfway through the planning, one of my colleagues pointed out to me that because of this company's particular viewpoint, it would be better off for us not to present in our normal way.

Initially, this threw me a little bit. I was naturally quite happy at the idea of doing something that I was comfortable with, but I quickly realised that my colleague was correct, and changed my approach. I decided to take a completely different outlook on the project, and produce something with a bit more creative flair. I knew that this was a big risk to take, but I believed that it was the right one given the circumstances, and that our normal style of presentation would not have worked. I was happy to change my way of working, with the goal of the team in mind. When I explained my new idea to the team, they all thought it was great, and praised me for my quick innovation and on-the-spot thinking.

We got to work, and ultimately produced a brilliant presentation. The partnership agency were extremely impressed, and ultimately invested even more money than we had hoped for. As a result, my managers were full of praise for both myself and my team.'

Sample Question 2

Q. Tell me about a time when you have demonstrated your emotional awareness.

How To Answer

Again, this is very straightforward question. Here the interview is asking you to demonstrate when you have shown the core competency of emotional awareness. Remember that emotional awareness does not just apply to being emotionally aware of the feelings of others, but of your own feelings too. You must be able to control your emotions when under high amounts of pressure, and exhibit strong levels of decision making.

Write your answer to this question in the box below, and then compare it to our sample response:

Sample Response

'During my previous role as an administration manager, at my previous company, I was given leadership of a team of other admin workers. Our responsibilities included dealing with absences from the company, managing the finance elements of the business, and making appointments for the management team.

As the leader of the team, one of my jobs was to make sure that new staff to the department felt welcomed and integrated. On the week in question, we had two new staff members. One of them, named Eileen, was ultra-confident. She seemed very happy to take on any new tasks, and was happy to work independently. The other new staff member, named Maisie, was less confident. She seemed extremely nervous, and I got the impression that she would need quite a lot of help integrating to the department.

Although I very much wanted to keep an eye on both of them, I decided that I wanted to prioritise Maisie. Therefore, I asked another staff member if they would be happy to oversee Eileen's initial training – just to make sure that she was getting on okay. I then sat down with Maisie myself, to talk with her about integrating into the company. I calmly and professionally discussed her feelings about joining the company, about the work that she'd be doing, and the parts that she felt least confident about. Maisie confessed to me that she felt extremely nervous about the work, and didn't feel confident at all. I informed her that I totally understood her feelings, and assured her that it's completely normal to be nervous when you first start at a company.

Upon establishing which parts she was the least confident in, I put together an action plan. This included training on certain areas, and I also offered to run through certain elements of the job with her as she was doing them, to get her confident in the role.

We worked together for a period of three days, after which time Maisie felt confident enough to work on her own. I am pleased to say that she did really well after this, and was an exemplary member of our team.'

Sample Question 3

Q. Can you give me an example of a time when you have worked as part of a team, to solve a problem?

How To Answer

The core competency being assessed in this question is obviously 'working collaboratively.' However, you will notice that they haven't directly used the competency (or at least the wording) in the question. This is something that you need to be ready for, because it's a common interview technique that's used to trip you up. Your job is to assess which competency the question is asking for in this case, and then produce a great answer. Teamwork is a fundamental part of working as a police officer, and the better you can work as part of a collaborative unit, the better level of service you can provide to the public. Good police work is about building partnerships, not just with your colleagues, but with members of the public too. You must be polite and respectful with every person that you meet, and show that the police value the ideals of teamwork, collaboration and social unity.

Write your answer to this question in the box below, and then compare it to our sample response:

Sample Response

'Whilst working for my previous company, as a member of the events team, I was part of the group responsible for managing and organising company conferences. In order to do this, we would have to make contact with the owners of the venue, as well as our client, and negotiate factors such as cost, availability and catering.

The event in question was to be a large-scale conference. Our client was an international refurbishment company, who were running the conference in order to enhance their business network. There were going to be over 500 people attending this conference, from all around the world, so it was essential that we got it right!

The first thing I did was to contact the manager of our client company. I asked him to provide me with a list of every single attendee, where they were travelling from, and whether they would have any special requirements. After the manager sent this through, I split the list into 5 separate parts – with 100 people being sent to 5 different teams within our department. I felt that this was the best approach to managing such a huge number of people. At all times, we liased with the other teams, to make sure everyone was on the right track.

Next, I contacted another department in our company, who were in charge of dealing with issues such as reviews and feedback. I asked them to provide me with the feedback we'd had on our past events, so that I could make sure we did the same things right, and improved on any weak areas. Once they provided me with this list, I made it a priority to improve on the areas which had received negative feedback.

Following the event, which was a huge success, I arranged a meeting with the manager of our client company, to get their thoughts on how the event was run. I wanted to make sure that we worked with this client, in a collaborative fashion, to run future events. The client seemed very happy with how the event was run, and provided us with sustained feedback – which we took into account for the future.'

Sample Question 4

Q. Describe a time when you have assumed responsibility for resolving a difficult problem, and taken steps to amend the issue.

How To Answer

Again, this question doesn't necessarily use the core competency in the wording, but the core competency to use here is 'taking ownership.' In order to work as a police officer, it's vital that you can take ownership and responsibility, and hold yourself accountable for your own actions. Part of this means accepting that sometimes minor mistakes will happen, but the way you deal with these is what is important. You must learn from your mistakes, and seek improvement-based feedback. Furthermore, it's critical that you can take pride in your work, and recognise your own limitations.

Write your answer to this question in the box below, and then compare it to our sample response:

Sample Response

'In my previous role, I worked as a team leader at a catering company. The company had a great reputation, and are well-known nationally.

Our company would be paid to organise the catering for parties and events, with different events being given to different teams within the organisation. As one of the team leaders, my role was to oversee the management of any projects that my team was given. This included making sure that the budget was kept to, motivating staff to perform at their best, and giving my team instructions on how we should allocate our resources. In order to help me manage the team, I had assigned a sub-team leader, named Michelle. Michelle would essentially act as my deputy, and would be given responsibility for taking key decisions.

On the day in question, we were preparing for an event in Wolverhampton. The event in question was a big birthday party. I sent my team to the venue to help start setting up, whilst I met with the person who was running the event, just to crosscheck on key elements such as time, and food allergy requirements. When I arrived at the venue, I found that two members of the team were engaged in a furious debate. One of them was Michelle. Voices were being raised and things were getting extremely heated. This was attracting the attention of the venue staff, who looked extremely unimpressed by the situation.

I quickly stepped across, and asked Michelle and the other team member to calm down and come with me outside, so that we could resolve this. I then calmly and professionally asked them to explain what the issue was. Michelle explained to me that the team member in question was refusing to obey her instructions. She had asked him to lay out a series of fish pasties across the table on the right-hand side, but he had refused.

Upon hearing this, the team member furiously interrupted. He said that we shouldn't be serving fish pasties, because some attendees would be allergic to fish. He referred to Michelle in extremely demeaning terms.

Having spoken with the event manager, I was fully aware of all allergy requirements – and none of the attendees were allergic to fish.

After listening to the complaints, I first addressed the team member. I explained to him that the way he had spoken to Michelle was completely unacceptable, and that even if she had made a mistake then this would not be okay. I then explained to him that he was in fact wrong, and there were no attendees who were allergic. To back this up, I showed him the event listing, which contained the details of all known allergies.

Once the team member saw this, he acknowledged that he had made a mistake, and apologised profusely to Michelle. He begged me not to fire him. Michelle immediately accepted his apology, and informed him that mistakes happen, and that the important thing is to move forward and resolve this. I was happy with this, and authorised the team member to get back to work.

Following this, I spoke to Michelle and informed her that I was pleased with how she dealt with the situation, and that she was doing a great job.'

Sample Question 5

Q. Can you give me an example of a time when you have supported another person or individual?

How To Answer

This question falls under the competency of deliver, support and inspire. The question focuses mainly on the 'supporting' element of the competency, but you should try and get the other aspects in too! Remember that your positive contribution to the police is extremely important. Police officers must show an understanding of how their behaviour impacts on the reputation of the service, and strive to make a positive contribution to this at all times. You must be focused on helping your teammates to achieve high standards, whilst maintaining your own.

Write your answer to this question in the box below, and then compare it to our sample response:

Sample Response

'Whilst working in my previous role, as a sales assistant in a computer shop, I was required to use my technical expertise on a number of occasions.

One such incident occurred on a regular weekday. A customer had come into the store, to complain that the laptop he'd brought from us two months earlier, had crashed. The customer did not have warranty on this laptop. My colleague, who was new to the role, was assigned to deal with the customer.

Unfortunately, my colleague made a mistake, which resulted in the customer becoming very angry. In response, my colleague was very rude to the customer, demonstrating very poor customer handling skills.

After stepping in to defuse this situation, I apologised wholeheartedly on behalf of the store and offered the customer a full refund, or a replacement laptop, and he seemed happy with this.

Once the customer had left the store, I took my colleague to one side. He was extremely upset by the incident, and felt that he had let down our employers. I tried to stay positive and encouraged him not to feel upset about the incident, and to use it as a chance to grow, improve and deliver a great level of service next time. I found out that the individual in question had had almost zero customer service training before being placed on the shop floor, and this was likely the reason for his poor communication. I immediately explained to him exactly why customer service is so essential. I told him that he was a representative of the shop, and that the shop's reputation would be damaged by behaviour such as this. I also explained that we have a duty to customers to be polite and respectful at all times, even if we do not agree with what the customer is saying.

Finally, I reassured him that I was confident in his ability to do the job, and would always be here to help if he needed advice.

Following this incident, I noticed a marked increase in my colleague's behaviour. The next time he was placed in such a situation, he remained calm and composed, and exhibited a good level of service towards the customer.'

Sample Question 6

Q. Can you give me an example of a time when you have critically analysed a situation, to produce a positive outcome?

How To Answer

Pretty straightforward here, the question is obviously testing the core competency of analysing critically! Working as a police officer involves large amount of critical analysis. You'll be presented with a wide variety of data, and will need to use all of this data to come to informed decisions and utilise an 'evidence based approach'. You must be able to use all of the data available to you in an efficient and effective manner, gathering as many facts and hard info as possible, before using this data in the most logical way.

Write your answer to this question in the box below, and then compare it to our sample response:

Sample Response

'In my previous role, I was working as one of the management chefs at a prestigious restaurant chain. My role was to work within the kitchen, helping junior chefs to complete their orders on time and directing busy kitchen traffic, as well as managing lots of my own dishes. Naturally, this was a role which placed extensive responsibility on me, and was highly stressful. It was important to stay composed at all times, and maintain a clear head.

On one such occasion, we were in the middle of a busy shift, when one of the chefs suddenly became very ill. He was vomiting into the kitchen toilet, and clearly was unable to work. I sent him home immediately. Now, however, we had a big problem. If we replaced the chef in question, who was a specialist in his grill area, then we would have a gap elsewhere. I quickly analysed the situation and came up with a solution: myself and another staff member would share the workload of the missing chef, pitching in where necessary. I spoke to the team and they agreed with my solution. I immediately went to the front-of-house manager and explained the situation, but informed him that naturally this would put a slight delay on food times – whilst everyone pitched in and worked to overcome the problem. He seemed happy with this solution, and started informing customers.

Although it was really difficult, and we did struggle at times, the team managed to come out of the shift with our heads held high and a sense of comradery. We received thanks from the front-of-house manager for managing the situation so well, and all of the customers seemed happy with their food – which meant that we had not let our quality slip even in the face of adversity.

I strongly believe that my quick thinking and ability to analyse the situation contributed to this solution, and ensured that everything ran smoothly.'

The Final Interview

Some police constabularies will also ask you to attend a second interview, at their premises, where they'll ask you some extra questions. These questions will likely be a mix between competency-based questions and values questions.

The purpose of the final interview is to allow the service to ask you questions that are outside of the competencies that have been assessed at the assessment centre. In essence it allows the service to find out more about you, your application, your motivations for wanting to become a police officer, and what you know about the role and the service that you are applying to join.

The interview panel will normally consist of 2-3 people and is usually made up of uniformed police officers and also a member of the human resources team. The length of the interview will very much depend on the questions the panel want to ask you and also how long your responses are. In general terms the interview will normally last for approximately one hour.

There are a number of areas that you will need to prepare for and these are as follows:

1. Interview technique.

2. The reasons why you want to become a police officer and what you know about the role.

3. What you know about the service you are applying to join.

Now that we understand how to prepare for the interview, let us break down each particular section in detail.

INTERVIEW TECHNIQUE

Many candidates spend little or no time improving or developing their interview technique. It is important that you spend sufficient time on this area, as it will allow your confidence to improve.

The way to improve interview technique is to carry out what we call a mock interview. Mock interviews are where you ask a friend or relative to ask you a number of interview questions under formalised interview conditions. This can be achieved at home across your dining room table or even whilst sat on the chairs in your living room.

During the mock interview you should work on your interview technique. The mock interview will also give you a valuable opportunity to try out your responses to a number of sample interview questions that are contained within this guide. It is important that your mock interviewer provides you with constructive feedback. Do not choose somebody who will tell you that you were great, even when you weren't, as this just defeats the whole purpose of a mock interview.

CARRYING OUT A MOCK INTERVIEW

*   Choose a quiet room in the house or at another suitable location.

*   Set the room up with a table and two chairs.

*   The interviewer then invites you into the room and the interview commences. Don't forget to be polite and courteous to the interviewer and only sit down when invited to do so.

*   When the interviewer asks you the questions, respond to them in a logical manner and in a tone of voice that can be easily heard.

*   Throughout the mock interview work hard on your technique and style. Sit upright at all times and look at the interviewer using soft eye contact. Do not fidget or slouch in the interview chair.

*   Once the interview is over, ask the interviewer for feedback on your performance.

*   Repeat the process at least three times until you are comfortable with your technique and style of answering.

THE REASONS WHY YOU WANT TO BECOME A POLICE OFFICER AND WHAT YOU KNOW ABOUT THE ROLE

During the final interview the panel may ask you questions that relate to why you want to become a police officer and in particular what you know about the role.

In the build-up to your interview you need to think carefully about why you want to become a police officer and what it is exactly that has attracted you to the role. Those candidates who want to become a police officer so that they can 'catch criminals' and 'ride about in a police car with the blue lights flashing' will score poorly. Only you will know the exact reasons why you want to join the police but here are some examples of good reasons, and examples of poor reasons.

Good reasons to give:

• To make a difference to your community, make it a safer place and reduce any fear that the public may have.

• To carry out a job that is worthwhile and one that makes a difference.

• The variety of the job and the different challenges that you will face on a day-to-day basis.

• The chance to work with a highly professional team that is committed to achieving the values and principles of the service.

• The opportunity to learn new skills.

Poor reasons to give:

• The pay and pension.

• The leave or holiday that you will get.

• Wearing a uniform, which ultimately means you don't have to pay for your own work clothes.

• Catching criminals and driving a police car.

Now, let's look at some sample questions and answers!

SAMPLE QUESTION NUMBER 1

Q. Tell us why you want to become a police officer?

Sample response

"I have worked in my current role now for a number of years. I have an excellent employer and enjoy working for them but unfortunately no longer find my job challenging. I understand that the role of a police officer is both demanding and rewarding and I believe I have the qualities to thrive in such an environment. I love working under pressure, working as part of a team that is diverse in nature and helping people in difficult situations. The public expectations of the police are very high and I believe I have the right qualities to help the police deliver the right service to the community.

I have studied the police core competencies and believe that I have the skills to match them and deliver what they require."

Top tips

- Don't be negative about your current or previous employer.

- Be positive, enthusiastic and upbeat in your response.

- Make reference to the core competencies if possible.

SAMPLE QUESTION NUMBER 2

Q. Why have you chosen this particular Police Service?

Sample response

"I have carried out extensive research into the Police Service and in particular this constabulary. I have been impressed by the level of service it provides. The website provides the community with direct access to a different range of topics and the work that is being carried out through your community wardens is impressive. I have looked at the national and local crime statistics and read many different newspapers and articles.

I like this Police Service because of its reputation and the police officers that I have spoken to have told me that they get a great deal of job satisfaction from working here."

Top tips

- Research the service thoroughly and make reference to particular success stories that they have achieved.

- Be positive, enthusiastic and upbeat in your response.

- Be positive about their service and don't be critical of it, even if you think it needs improving in certain areas.

SAMPLE QUESTION NUMBER 3

Q. What does the role of a police officer involve?

Sample response

"Before I carried out my research and looked into the role of the police officer, I had the normal, stereotypical view of a police officer in that they catch criminals and reduce crime for a living.

Whilst there is an element of that in the job, the police officer's role is far more diverse and varied. For example, they are there to serve the community and reduce the element of fear. They do this by communicating with their communities and being visual wherever possible.

They may need to pay particular attention to a person or groups of people who are the victims of crime or hatred. Therefore the role of a police officer is to both physically and psychologically protect the community that they are serving.

It is also their role to work with other organisations such as the Fire Service, Social Services and other public sector bodies to try to reduce crime in a coordinated response as opposed to on their own."

Top tip

- Understand the police core competencies and be able to recite them word for word.

SAMPLE QUESTION NUMBER 4

Q. If one of the members of your team was gay and they told you this over a cup of tea at work, how do you think you would react?

Sample response

"I would have no problem at all. A person's sexual preference is their right and they should not be treated any differently for this. My attitude towards them and our working relationship would not be affected in any way. I have always treated everyone with respect and dignity at all times and will continue to do so throughout my career."

Top tip

- Understand everything there is to know about equality and fairness. If you do not believe in it then this job is not for you.

SAMPLE QUESTION NUMBER 5

Q. If you were given an order that you thought was incorrect would you carry it out?

Sample response

"Yes I would. I would always respect my senior officers and their decisions. However, if I thought something could be done in a better way then I do think that it is important to put it across, but in a structured and non-confrontational manner. During a debrief would probably be an appropriate time to offer up my views and opinions if asked but I would never refuse to carry out an order or even question it during an operational incident or otherwise."

SAMPLE QUESTION NUMBER 6

Q. What do you understand by the term equality and fairness?

Sample response

"It is an unfortunate fact that certain groups in society are still more likely to suffer from unfair treatment and discrimination. It is important for the Police Service and its staff to strive to eliminate all forms of unfair treatment and discrimination on the grounds that are specified in their policies or codes of practice.

Equality and fairness is the working culture in which fair treatment of all is the norm."

Top tips

- Try to read the Police Service's policy on equality and fairness. You may be able to find this by visiting their website or asking them for a copy of it to help you in your preparation.

- Consider reading the Race Relations Act, and understand the duties that are placed upon public sector organisations such as the police.

SAMPLE QUESTION NUMBER 7

Q. How do you think the police could recruit more people from ethnic minority groups?

Sample response

"To begin with it is important that Police Services continue to build effective public relations. This can be achieved through certain avenues such as the service's website or even the local press. If the Police Service has a community liaison officer then this would be a good way to break down any barriers in the communities that we want to recruit from.

Another option is to ask people from these specific groups how they view this Police Service and what they think we could do to recruit more people from their community. Along with this it may be an option to focus media campaigns where there are higher populations of ethnic minority groups."

COMPREHENSIVE LIST OF INTERVIEW QUESTIONS TO PREPARE FOR

Q. Why do you want to become a police officer?

Q. What are your strengths?

Q. What are your weaknesses?

Q. What can you tell us about this particular Police Service?

Q. What do you understand by the term 'teamwork'?

Q. What makes an effective team?

Q. Why would you make a good police officer?

Q. What do you think the role of a police officer entails?

Q. If you saw a colleague being bullied or harassed, what would you do?

Q. What do you think the qualities of an effective police officer are?

Q. If one of your colleagues told you that they were gay, how would you react?

Q. What have you done so far to find out about the role of a police officer?

Q. Why do you want to join this particular Police Service?

Q. Give examples of when you have had to work as a team.

Q. What would you do if a member of your team was not pulling their weight or doing their job effectively?

Q. Have you ever had to diffuse a confrontational situation? What did you do and what did you say?

Q. What are the main issues affecting the police at this current time?

Q. What do you understand about the term 'equality and fairness'?

Q. What do you understand by the term 'equal opportunities'?

Q. If you ever heard a racist or sexist remark, what would you do?

Q. Would you say that you are a motivated person?

Q. How do you keep yourself motivated?

Q. Have you ever had to work as part of a team to achieve a common goal?

Q. If you were in the canteen at work and two senior officers began to make homophobic comments, what would you do?

Q. Have you ever made a poor decision? If so, what was it?

Q. If you were ever given an order that you thought was incorrect what would you do?

Q. Have you ever had to work with somebody that you dislike?

Q. What is wrong with your current job? Why do you want to leave it to become a police officer?

Q. Have you ever carried out a project from beginning to end?

Q. How do you think you would cope with the anti-social working hours?

Q. Have you ever had to work shifts?

Q. How do you think you would cope with working the police shift system?

What Happens Next?

After a short wait, the police will contact you to let you know how you got on. They will send you a feedback report form, which details how you scored in each area of the assessment centre, things you did well and things you didn't do so well. Then, it's on to the second assessment day!

Police Officer Assessment:
Day Two

Following day one, you will be invited to attend a second assessment day, where you will undergo various medical and fitness checks. When and where you do this will depend very much on the constabulary that you are applying to.

Fitness is extremely important when working in the police. It's imperative that police officers can demonstrate that they are up to the physical demands of the job. When working as a police officer, there are times when you will be required to catch criminals or even use physical force, which means that you'll be pushed to the limits of your exertion. Furthermore, a healthy body leads to a healthy mind.

The fitness test stage of the police selection process covers two specific areas.

These are as follows:

- The Endurance Test or Multi Stage Fitness Test.

- The Dynamic Strength Test.

On the following pages we have provided you with information relating to each of the two individual sections, but it is important that you check with the service you are applying to join that the information is correct.

The police fitness test is not too difficult but obviously this will very much depend on your own abilities. With a degree of focused preparation you can pass the police fitness test with relative ease.

You may also wish to purchase the actual endurance test/bleep test audio CD from our online shop how2become.com.

This CD is a very similar to the test used by the police and you will find it a useful tool in your preparation.

THE ENDURANCE TEST

The endurance test, also known as the 'multi-stage fitness test', 'bleep' or 'shuttle run' test, is often used by sports coaches and trainers to estimate an athlete's VO2 Max (maximum oxygen uptake). Apart from the police, the test is also used by the Armed

Forces, Emergency Services and Prison Service as part of their selection process but it is also a great way to improve and monitor your own fitness level.

The 'bleep' test involves running continuously between two points that are 15 metres apart (20 metres in some cases). These 'shuttle' runs are done in time to pre-recorded 'bleep' sounds on an audio CD or cassette. The time between the recorded 'bleeps' decreases after each minute and therefore the test becomes progressively harder with each level completed. The full test consists of approximately 23 levels but the actual police endurance test only requires you to achieve 4 shuttles at level 5 to pass. Each level lasts approximately 60 seconds.

A level is basically a series of 15 metre 'shuttle runs'. The starting speed is normally 8.5 km/hr, which then increases by 0.5km/hr with each new level.

To purchase your copy of the bleep test please visit www.How2Become.com.

THE DYNAMIC STRENGTH TEST

This test mimics a seated bench press action and a seated rowing action. You will be asked to perform 5 repetitions on both the push and pull aspects. The machine works out the average of your 5 repetitions and gives you a score. You must push 34kg and pull 35kg to pass.

Two of the most effective ways to prepare for this type of test include rowing (using a rowing machine) and press ups. The reason why we recommend rowing during your preparation is that apart from increasing your physical strength it will also help prepare you for the endurance test.

IMPORTANT: Make sure you consult a medical practitioner prior to engaging in any strenuous physical exercise program.

Following the fitness test, you will need to complete a medical assessment with the police. The medical assessment will test you on areas such as:

Vision – using both eyes, you must be 6/6 in order to pass. This part of the test accepts the use of glasses or contact lenses. You will be tested unaided too, and must not be less than 6/36 for this.

BMI – You must have a BMI of 32 or lower, or less than 30% body fat for men, and less than 36% body fat for women.

You've now reached the end of *How To Become A Police Officer*. By using this book, you've given yourself a huge boost in your chances of successfully joining the Police Service. However, now the onus is on you. You must take the tips in this book and apply them. You need to work hard, and put the effort in, before you can achieve success.

When applying for the police, keep the following in mind:

1. Preparation. Preparation is key to passing any job selection process – you won't be doing yourself any favours by not taking the time to prepare. Many people fail because they did not know what to expect or did not know what their own weaknesses were. Take the time to go over any areas you may have struggled with. By doing this, you will become familiar with how you will perform when it comes to the assessment centre.

2. Perseverance. If you set your sights on a goal and stick to it, you are more likely to succeed. Obstacles and setbacks are common when trying to achieve something great, and you shouldn't shy away from them. Instead, face the tougher parts even if you feel defeated. If you need to, take a break from your work to relax and then return with renewed vigour. If you fail a particular part of the selection process, take the time to consider why you failed, gather your strength and try again.

3. Performance. How well you perform will be the result of your preparation and perseverance. Remember to relax when taking the tests and try not to panic. Believe in your own abilities, practise as much as you can, and motivate yourself constantly. Nothing is gained without hard work and determination, and this applies to the police as much as anything else in life.

We wish you the best of luck in all of your future endeavours!

The how2become team

The How2Become Team

WANT FURTHER HELP PASSING THE SELECTION PROCESS? CHECK OUT OUR OTHER GUIDES:

FOR MORE INFORMATION CHECK OUT THE FOLLOWING:

WWW.HOW2BECOME.COM

Get Access To
FREE
Psychometric
Tests

www.PsychometricTestsOnline.co.uk